A Duffer's Guide to
BETTER GOLF

A Simplified Approach to Getting the Most from Your Game

David Iwanaga

**Published by
Eagle Publishing**

DUFFER

duf-fer \'dəf-ər\ *n* [origin unknown]
1   **a** : an incompetent, ineffectual, or clumsy person   **b** : ineffective player of golf; *slang.*

*Dedicated to all those who strive
to play this non-violent game
violently within.*

A Duffer's Guide to Better Golf
A Simplified Approach to Getting the Most from Your Game

by David Iwanaga

Copyright © 1997 Eagle Publishing
Eagle Publishing, P.O. Box 14118
Pinedale, CA 93650

Special thanks to:

Bruce Lee, Tao of Jeet Kune Do (Ohara Publications, Inc., Santa Clarita, CA 1975) Copyright © 1975 by Linda Lee. Reprinted by permission of the publisher.

Tommy Armour, How to Play Your Best Golf All the Time (Simon & Schuster, New York, NY 1953) Copyright © 1953 by Thomas D. Armour, copyright renewed (c) 1981 by John Armour and Benjamin Andrews. Reprinted by permission of the publisher.

Printed in U.S.A.

Library of Congress Catalog Card Number: .96-096384

ISBN 0-9652517-6-4

10 9 8 7 6 5 4 3 2 1

Softcover $15.95

Illustrations: Steve Austin
Cover Design: Jeff Austin
Photos: Jim Koike
Editing: Gail Kearns
Golf Model: Jim Perez
Fitness Model: Karen Gerdts

TABLE OF CONTENTS

Disclaimer . . .

This book is the author's own opinions and views on the game of golf. Golf is an athletic activity that requires one to have achieved a certain level of fitness before proceeding with the exercises and techniques presented in this manual. It is sold with the understanding that the publisher and author are not liable for any injuries or damage caused by the reader playing or practicing golf.

The purpose of this book is to provide information and entertainment. The author and Eagle Publishing shall have neither liability nor responsibility to any person or entity with respect to any loss or damage caused, or alleged to be caused, directly or indirectly by the information contained in this book.

If you do not wish to be bound by the above, you may return this book to the publisher for a full refund.

CHAPTER ONE

INTRODUCTION
Martial Arts & Golf

"The outstanding characteristic of the expert athlete is his ease of movement, even during maximal effort. The novice is characterized by his tenseness, wasted motion and excess effort. That rare person, the *natural athlete,* seems to be endowed with the ability to undertake any sport activity, whether he is experienced in it or not, with ease. The ease is his ability to perform with minimal antagonistic tension. It is more present in some athletes than in others, but can be improved by all."[1]

The great martial artist Bruce Lee made his craft look effortless. He demonstrated how precise timing and relaxation

---

1: Bruce Lee, <u>Tao of Jeet Kune Do</u> (Ohara Publications, Copyright 1975)

in his movements created incredible power and speed. By making his movements very natural to his body, he created his own style that was *most effective for him.* He understood the concept of *economy of motion.* When we observe top PGA pros, they swing with minimal effort, yet strike the ball with power and accuracy. When we observe most amateurs, they swing with maximum effort, yet strike the ball with inconsistent results.

The concepts and techniques of the martial arts are directly related to the techniques used to play the game of golf. From the mental aspects of focus and concentration to the physical aspects of speed and timing, golf is a form of martial arts. Karate techniques, which translates to "empty hands", are based on the *natural movements* of animals: the power and grace of the tiger; the balance and fluidity of the crane; the lightning strike and speed of the cobra; the quickness and evasiveness of the mongoose. *The swing of a golfer?* Sounds a bit ludicrous, but it's not as crazy as you might think. Think about the first time you picked up a rock and threw it, or the first time you threw a baseball. If you are right-handed, you probably cocked your right arm back, turned your body with your back to the target and wound yourself up like a spring while transferring your weight to your right foot. When you got wound up as tight as you could go, you gradually released that energy and let your hips unwind while your weight began to transfer forward. The unwinding of your hips pulled your torso around as the speed built up and your shoulders squared, pulling your arm around with your right elbow moving toward the target and aligning your hand just before it whipped through sending the ball hurling to its destination as your weight fully transferred to your left foot and you finish in a balanced position. Your objective was the target; you did not have to think about the technique to get it there—you just did it! Well, you just made the perfect golf swing!

Golf is fast becoming the world's most popular sport. As an accomplished martial artist and fellow golf enthusiast, I have been bitten by the "golf bug" and strive to improve my game every day. In 1976, when I began studying Shou' Shu' Karate, I began to analyze all the movements I learned in class and tried to make sense of why they work. I used to wonder how those "little karate guys" could hit so hard with so much speed! As I became more proficient, I realized that in martial arts there is very little wasted movement or effort. Every movement builds upon the previous one and has a definite purpose. When this economy of movement and timing is developed, you not only become faster but also more powerful; we call this ki'. To develop your golfing ki', it is important to understand the basis of the movements for the golf swing.

If you're like most golf enthusiasts, you probably do not get a chance to play more than once a week unless perhaps you sneak off to the range in between. With the limited amount of time we practice and play, our progress to "Golf Heaven" is much slower than we would like. This book will help you learn how to build your game around your own ki' which is innate inside each one of us.

From the day I first picked up the clubs, I became a golf junkie. I dove into it with my eyes wide open; I tried to learn everything I could about the game. After taking numerous classes offered at local ranges; private lessons from several different instructors; attending the prestigious Golf University in Rancho Bernardo, California; viewing every video on the shelf; reading just about every how-to book and publication there was, I considered myself a real student of the game. After studying and analyzing all the materials, what I came away with was *much confusion*.

It seems that everybody has their own theory on the golf

swing. With all the different steps to the swing, the various positions of the ball, arms, feet, angles of the body, the different sequence of movements, it's no wonder golf is also one of the most difficult and frustrating sports. But much of the frustration comes from thinking about the swing too much.

SWING THOUGHTS

When we watch the tour pros play, they make the game look easy. But the expert athlete in any sport makes the difficult look easy. Do you remember the first time you strapped on a pair of skates or a pair of skis? The first time I put on a pair of skis, I remember thinking, "Man was not made to go down a snow covered mountain with his feet strapped to two boards." Skiing, like golf, is one of those sports we tend to rely on friends advice about, rather than taking proper lessons. But skiing is very tactile and your body learns to react to conditions and commands largely through feedback from your skis to your brain. With skiing, though, it is a matter of survival; you can get hurt if you go at it blindly. With golf, it is more of a matter of embarrassment and frustration.

We amateurs like to just go for it when we take on a new endeavor; we never seem to take proper lessons. Sometimes we are successful, but with golf many techniques used in a proper swing are opposite of everything we learned growing up: hit down to go up; swing easy to go long; aim right to go left. I used to think there was an exact science to the golf swing and any deviation from that science would influence my results. Most teaching materials I've examined are geared in that regard. There are two problems with this approach:

1. *Humans are very "hands on;" we use our hands anytime we feel we need to control actions.* For most amateurs, using one's hands to control a golf swing is the "kiss of death" to making a good swing!

2. *Humans are all different.* To expect the same swing to work for each of us is ridiculous. Our bodies and temperaments are different, so what works for one might not work for the other.

Golf is a technical sport, but it is a very tactile game that is best developed around one's own temperament. You have to listen to your body. From the feedback it gives you, learn to develop your game. If you watch some of the great players like Nicklaus, Trevino, and Floyd, these guys all have a unique and non-textbook swing. The one thing they have in common is that they have developed their respective swings over the years with what works for them. This book is designed to help you find your own *natural swing*. We are all different; our swings should be as natural and individual as we are. You can be bombarded with books and tapes of techniques and swing theories; some might work but many will just confuse your situation. If you allow your body to do what it wants to do and try not to force it into an awkward movement, you will gain consistency and confidence in your swing. By simplifying the steps to finding your *natural golf swing*, you can concentrate on making the shots, not making the swing.

This book also encourages amateurs to change the way they mentally approach the game. Nothing slows improvement like frustration and embarrassment. The statement "*the harder you try, the more you are bound to fail,*" is absolutely true in the game of golf! Remember why you play the game. Most of you are not playing this sport to make a living, you *play to relax and have fun*! So stop beating yourself up, play the game the way it was supposed to be played and have fun.

CHAPTER TWO

GOLF FITNESS
Exercise & Golf

Many think that golf is not a sport—just a retired persons game—that you do not have to be in shape to play. While it's true that your fitness level does not have to be that of a professional athlete, you will see greater results in the progress and enjoyment of your game if you are in shape, especially golf-shape.

Do you ever wake up with sore muscles the day after you play a round? How about if you take on one of those giant buckets of balls at the range? Do you ever labor to finish 18 holes on a warm day? How about if you do not take a cart? Being physically fit and flexible are important components to maximizing your playing potential.

To enjoy the game and play at your best, golfers should prepare themselves physically. Two things can actually help the average golfer:

1. Get in shape, especially golf shape.

2. Walk the course when you are allowed.

Most people walk over five miles on and around a golf course during a round.

I have heard of many people hurting their backs due to swinging a golf club. You can still play great golf without being a rubberband. Many players have learned to generate clubhead speed by other means. Arnold Palmer has what many refer to as a *muscular swing*. Flexibility is the key to acquiring a long swing arc that is so essential for developing clubhead speed for length off the tee. If you watch the current long hitters on the tour such as Greg Norman, Ernie Els, Davis Love III, and John Daly, they all produce a long swing arc with a big shoulder turn that requires great flexibility. Watch the individuals that play on tours. Those players are athletes demonstrating great flexibility, timing and power. *The full golf swing is a very athletic move.* It is important to be fit and flexible not just to play golf, but to achieve *a healthier and less stressful life.*

To develop a fluid-like and powerful swing, flexibility is important to help prepare your body and help prevent injuries that can come from twisting and turning your body during a swing. Somebody is always saying that they have been lifting weights, and this has ruined their golf swing. It's not that bigger muscles inhibit the golf swing, it's that most people who push heavy weights fail to stretch properly. When I began studying martial arts, my karate instructor was a fourth degree black belt who possessed great flexibility, speed and power.

He lifted heavy weights—enough to produce a four hundred-pound bench press but maintained his flexibility and speed through martial arts. John Daly is a big guy, but I do not think there is anybody on the tour who possesses the flexibility that he does.

There are many ways to attain better flexibility:

1. *Get a massage:* Believe it or not, some of us have muscles that have been sitting around getting tight from tension and stress. It is amazing how much more the muscles relax from a proper massage. A relaxed muscle is much easier to stretch than a tensed one.

2. *Take a yoga class:* I found yoga not only to be great for stretching, but also great for learning how to relax. A relaxed body not only enhances the smoothness and release of your golf swing, but helps you get rid of those first tee jitters caused by the twenty swing—thoughts you take to the first tee.

3. *Exercise:* I'm not suggesting that you start a strict regimen of aerobic and anaerobic exercises, but simply stretching a little each day helps prepare you to play golf.

The following exercises will help you achieve not only a smoother swing, but also a healthier and less stressful life. [2]

To properly stretch your muscles, they must first be warmed up. Warm up by running in place or performing jumping jacks for at least two minutes. *Important: When stretching a muscle, pull to a maximum permissible tension level and hold. Do not forget to breathe, and never bounce! Bouncing can cause a pull or worse, a tear.*

Note: Before beginning any new exercise program, please consult your physician.

[2]: I wish to acknowledge the Golf University of Rancho Bernardo, California and the The Yoga Center of Fresno, California for many of the exercises.

ARM CIRCLES

Make 20 small circles in each direction, 10 with palms up, 10 with palms down.

SHOULDER BLADE SPREAD

While standing, grab your shoulder blades as if you were hugging yourself. Lean forward, drop your chin to your chest, and exhale. Hold this position for 10 to 15 seconds. Repeat several times. *This will help relieve tension in your back.*

INTERIOR CUFF STRETCH

Reach over to the middle of your back, with the other hand grab the elbow and slowly pull down and hold for 30 seconds. Repeat with opposite arm. *Helps stretch back of arms.*

EXTERIOR CUFF STRETCH

Stand erect with your feet shoulder width apart. Hold your left arm straight out, then take your right hand and place it behind your left elbow. Try to pull the inside of your left arm toward your right shoulder. *Stretches upper back from spine.*

FRONT LAT. STRETCH

Interlace your fingers behind your head, push your elbows back as far as possible still touching your head. Take a deep breath in, lean back and hold for 10 seconds. Repeat twice. *Stretches lateral muscles.*

REJUVENATING BREATH

Slowly raise your arms over your head, take a deep breath as you lean back placing your hands on your kidneys. As you slowly exhale, start leaning forward letting your arms & head drop until your body is relaxed completely expelling your lungs. *Loosens and stretches back muscles.*

INVERTED POSITION TO PLOW

Lie down and raise your feet straight up. Prop your hips up in the air by placing your elbows flat on the ground and support your hips with your hands. Hold that position for a minute or two, then slowly let your feet come over your head stretching your back and neck. Hold this position for as long as comfortable. *This position takes time and should be done slowly, it may take weeks to obtain this position.*

CAT STRETCH

Exhale and arch back downward holding your head up, then inhale and arch back upward as your head drops between your arms stretching your neck. Repeat 10 times. *This loosens up the whole back.*

SIDE LYING TORSO STRETCH

Lie flat on your back with your arms out, pull your knees up with your lower leg parallel to the ground, then let your knees fold over to each side. Hold this position until your knees settle to the floor, then repeat this on the other side. *This helps the rotation of your lower back.*

ROTATIONAL TRUNK STRETCH

Sit flat on the floor with your legs out, cross your left foot over your right knee, look over your right shoulder while bracing your left elbow against your left knee, and pull as far as you can to the right and hold position for 30 seconds for each side. *This helps rotation of your upper back.*

COBRA

Lay face down flat on the ground, place your hands and forearms flat on the ground. While keeping your hips on the ground, raise your head up and look to the ceiling while pressing up arching your back. Hold for about 20 seconds. *This stretches your lower back.*

FALLEN LEAF

Get on your knees with toes pointed and legs slightly spread, sit on your ankles, bend forward with your hands at your side, palms up, try to lay the side of your face on the ground completely relaxing. *This will completely relax your back and shoulders.*

HARE

From the fallen leaf position, turn your head so that your
forehead is on the ground, turn your feet so you're on your
toes, then grab your heels. Push hard with your legs against
your hands as you roll the top of your head on the ground.
You should feel the pull on your shoulders and upper back.
Stretches shoulder and back muscles.

HAMSTRING STRETCH

Stand erect, cross your right foot over your left foot placing them next to each other, edge to edge. Slowly try to reach for your toes, holding this position for 20 seconds, then reverse. *Stretches hamstrings and calves.*

CAT POSITION

Start on your hands and knees, roll on your toes, raise your hips up as you straighten your legs. Try to set your heels on the ground with straight legs as you let your head drop. Walk your hands back toward your feet, until eventually you are standing while grabbing your ankles. *This will stretch your back and the back of your legs.*

ARCH

Lay flat on your back, palms down, feet flat on the floor.
Now keeping your hands and feet on the ground, raise your
hips as high as they go and hold for 20 seconds. *This will
strengthen your lower back and buttocks.*

HURDLERS STRETCH

Sit flat on the ground, left leg straight out, right leg perpendicular to the left with the inside of the right knee and ankle flat on the ground. Grab your left foot and slowly try to pull your nose to your left knee. Hold for 15 seconds, grab your right knee and slowly try to pull your nose to your right knee. Hold for 15 seconds then switch legs. *This stretches the hamstring, lower back and groin.*

GROIN STRETCH

Sit flat on the ground, legs spread out as wide as possible. Grab your left foot, and slowly try to pull your nose to your left knee. Grab both feet and slowly try to pull your nose to the ground between your legs. Grab your right foot and slowly try to pull your nose to your knee. Hold each of these positions for about 15 seconds with constant pull. *This will stretch out your groin muscles.*

QUADRICEPS STRETCH

Stand facing a wall with your feet flat on the ground. Slowly raise your right leg toward your buttocks, reach down with your right hand and grab your ankle. Slowly pull the leg up as high as you can stretching the top of your leg and hold for 20 seconds. Repeat on other side. *This will stretch the quadriceps muscles.*

KNEE CRADLE

Lay on your back with your knees up, feet on the ground. Cross your right ankle over your left knee, grab behind your left leg, and slowly pull back toward your face. Hold for 30 seconds and repeat on other side. *This will stretch upper hamstring, groin and gluts.*

LEG BOUNCE

Sit on the ground with your legs out, lean back on your hands. Then keeping your heel in touch with the ground, let your legs bounce up and down for 30 seconds. *This will loosen up your leg muscles.*

STATIC BACK PRESS

Lay flat on your back with your legs elevated up on a sofa or chair. Close your eyes, take deep breaths, and relax in this position until your lower back settles to the floor. *This will completely relax your back.*

CHAPTER THREE

GOLF PHYSICS
How it Works

There are a lot of dynamics that happen during the golf swing. It is important to understand the physics of what happens to the clubhead and shaft from the backswing, to the downswing, to contact and follow—through. It is also important to understand what happens to the golf ball at impact, and the effects of off-center hits on the clubface to the ball flight. Understanding the basic physics of golf will help you to select the proper equipment, and give reason behind the swing theories developed later in the book. You should understand the principles behind the lessons that are taught. What's the first thing that every instructor, book or video has told you about swinging the club?

Keep the club on plane and swing from the inside.

Your swing path must be inside-out! Have you ever wondered why this is so? First, let's take a look at the design of a golf club as it reacts to the swing. When you set up behind the ball, the clubface is square to your target. As you take the clubhead back with relaxed arms, the toe of the club begins to rotate clockwise and should point straight up by the halfway position. As you swing down, the clubhead rotates counter-clockwise and is square at impact. As you allow the club to follow through, the clubhead continues to rotate until the toe is pointing down to the ground and your momentum takes you to a finish position. This slapping of the golf ball creates an additional force that helps create power in the shot. When this rotating (counter-clockwise) clubhead contacts the golf ball, the ball tends to come off the face with a clock-wise spin.

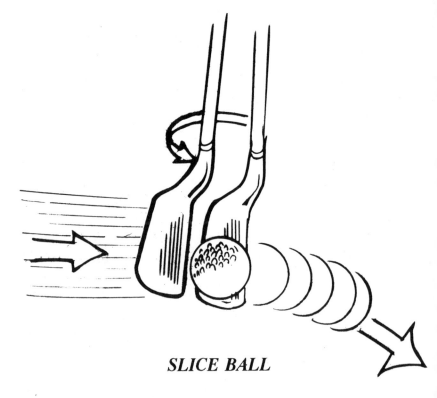

SLICE BALL

To compensate for this sideways spinning of the ball, the clubhead must approach the ball from inside the swing plane. The inside angle approach balances out the counter-clockwise rotation of the clubface. The term square-to-square in the golf swing that some instructors keep using is contradictory to the design intent of the clubhead.

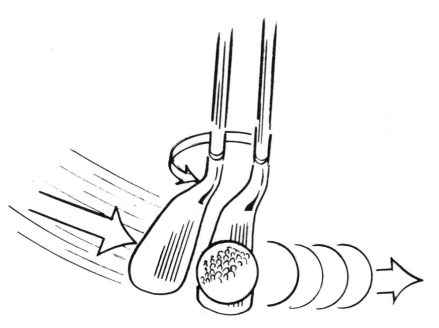

STRAIGHT BALL

By bringing the clubhead from the inside, the inside-out swing path will negate the outside-in clubhead turn creating a straight shot.

Keep a quiet lower body! The first thing I notice about high-handicappers versus low-handicappers is that high-handicappers swing with much more effort. My first golf instructor, Jim Perez, hits the ball a country mile with very little effort—at least it looks that way. Being your typical male golfer, all I wanted was to outdrive my buddies and really didn't care how I did it. I signed up for private lessons with Jim so I could learn to drive the ball like him. The first thing he did was to videotape my swing; he also videotaped his own using my clubs. When we viewed the tapes, it was apparent I was shifting my hips back and forth while Jim was keeping very still. I was concentrating so hard on making a big swing-arc and shifting my weight, I over-emphasized the swing movements. With my shifting hips and *over-active* lower body, I never had a solid base for my swing. My drives were all over the place, and Jim's were long and straight; well, at least I know it was not my clubs.

Think back to your fourth grade science class. Do you remember that washer on the end of a string with the other end tied to the tip of a pencil? As you spun the washer around with the pencil, you probably noticed that the less you moved the pencil, the faster the washer spun. It spun very fast when the axis of rotation was hardly moving. This same law of physics translates to the golf swing; *clubhead speed is developed through a quiet lower body.*

SWING AROUND A POINT

OPPOSITE THINKING

Hit down on the ball to go up! When hitting your irons, you must hit down on the ball to produce backspin in order to obtain height and accuracy in your shot.   This not only controls trajectory, but a skilled player can also control the roll distance after the ball hits the green. When the club takes a divot out of the grass, *that* divot should be made after the ball is in the air.

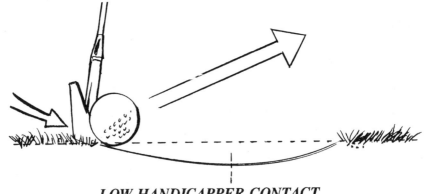

LOW-HANDICAPPER CONTACT

A ball struck with a downward blow possesses a rising trajectory that seems to drop the ball out of the sky on the green.

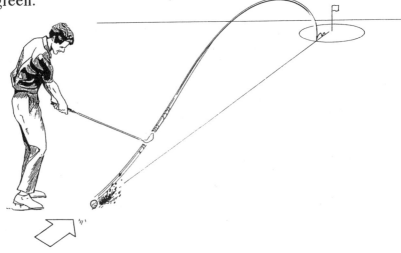

Most amateurs think they are suppose to hit the ground first and scoop the ball up.

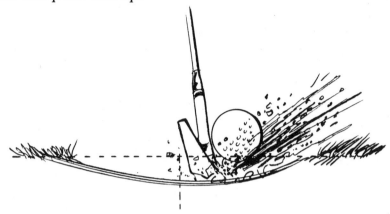

HIGH-HANDICAPPER CONTACT

A ball struck with a upward blow will produce inconsistent results. If you hit it thick, the ball flies short. If you hit it thin, the ball flies low and usually long. If you top it, the ball rolls pitifully down the fairway. The mistake most amateurs make is to think that a lofted club is supposed to scoop the ball up in the air.

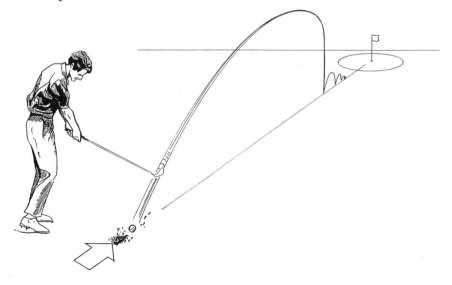

PHYSICS OF THE CLUB SHAFT

It is important to understand that the club shaft is not a stationary object. While it appears to be straight and stiff, a high speed film of it would reveal that the shaft bends back and forth quite a bit during a golf swing. The shaft loads on the downswing building power, then unloads at impact releasing power through the ball. The proper flex rating will synchronize this movement with your own golf swing. It is probably the most important and overlooked part of the club. If the shaft does not fit your swing, you will be penalized with bad golf shots.

BUILDING ENERGY

GOLF CLUB SHAFT LOADS ON DOWNSWING

As the club swings down, the shaft bends back building up power.   As the club approaches impact, the shaft should straightens itself unloading the stored power into the ball. The shaft accelerates through the impact zone and actually kicks the ball off the tee.   The problem most amateurs have is they feel they have to muscle the ball off the tee.   When you watch the pros, they swing the club smoothly and easily. They are allowing the club to do all the work. When the shaft is matched to your swing, the unloading of the shaft happens when it is supposed to.

RELEASING THE ENERGY

THE GOLF CLUB UNLOADING AT IMPACT

Aim to the left to fade the ball right! To fade the ball is easy for a high-handicapper. Recalling why we swing inside-out, we know that a swing plane other than that produces varying degrees of fade to the dreaded slice. If we stand more open to the target and square our clubface, the only possible way to swing the club is more outside-in creating a fade. This produces a clockwise spin resulting in a fade.

Aim to the right to draw the ball left! To draw the ball, you take a stance that is very closed to the target and square the club. This forces you to bring the club from way inside in order to make a swing. This inside-out path overcompensates the club's rotation and puts a counter-clockwise spin on the ball producing a draw.

CENTER OF GRAVITY

Most golfers are not familiar with how location of the clubheads center of gravity (c.g.) affects the trajectory of the ball and the performance of the club. Most clubs are designed with their center of gravity located in the middle of the club. Understanding the theories behind clubhead design can greatly help when selecting your golf equipment. The basic concept is: *Changing the club's center of gravity changes the trajectory of the ball.*

To hit the longest and straightest ball, you must contact the ball on the sweet spot or center of gravity of the clubface. When the club is struck off center, the club will try to twist around the center of gravity. This energy is not transmitted to the ball, it is wasted in the twisting motion resulting in a loss of distance. Perimeter weighted clubs are popular; they distribute the mass of the club around the perimeter enlarging the sweet spot. The perimeter-weighted club helps to ensure good distance even on off-center hits.

CAVITY BACKED IRONS

The principle here is simple; *the lower the center of gravity, the higher the trajectory of the ball.* For irons, lowering the center of gravity to Point B hits the ball higher with more backspin. Raising the center of gravity to Point C hits the ball lower with less spin. Point A is the typical center of gravity location on most irons.

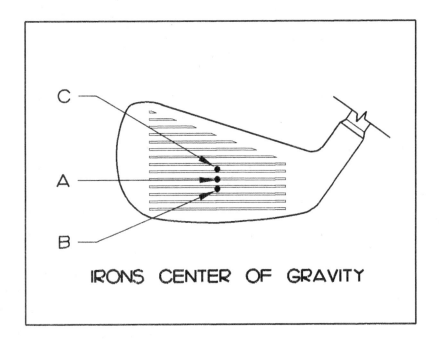

IRONS CENTER OF GRAVITY

If you've been having difficulty making solid contact with the ball, perhaps your club's center of gravity is not located where you think it is. To precisely locate the center of gravity, try using impact tape. This is tape you put on the clubface which leaves a clear impression where the ball is struck. When you make contact and hit the ball solidly, check to see where on the clubface you struck the ball. Repeat this several times until you are sure about the location of the sweet spot. With that in mind, you can move the center of gravity around your club by adding strips of lead tape in the desired direction. This, however, adds to the overall weight and change the flexing characteristics of the club. Many pros grind away metal to compensate for the added weight, keeping the club with the identical swing weight prior to modification. With woods, the principles are even more expanded. Moving the center of gravity around the clubface as well as in the depth of the clubhead affects the ball's action and trajectory. Most woods will hold their center of gravity on Point A. Hitting Point A hits the ball the straightest and farthest. By moving the c.g. to Point B, you hit more draws; moving to Point C, produces more fades. Moving to Point D, hits lower balls, while moving the c.g. to Point E, hits higher balls.

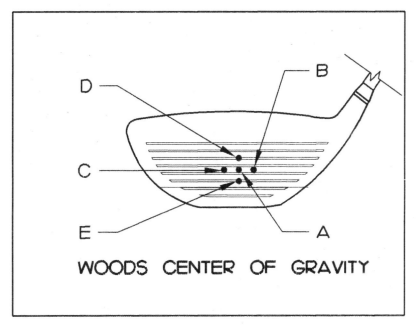

WOODS CENTER OF GRAVITY

The first persimmon-headed woods carried their center of gravity high and tended to hit a low ball. Brass soleplates were later added to lower the c.g. in order to hit a higher ball. Modern day metal headed drivers tend to carry their weight lower. This is why a current 9-degree driver hits about the same trajectory as an older 10.5-degree driver of wood. Also, changing the location of the c.g. in the body of the clubhead also affects the ball's trajectory. On most metal woods, Point A is typical. Moving the c.g. to Point B, hits a higher ball while moving to Point C, hits a lower ball.

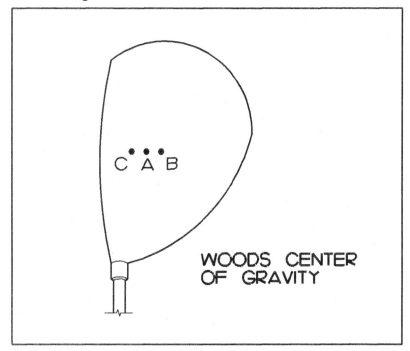

WOODS CENTER OF GRAVITY

Tests conducted by Titleist showed that lowering the c.g. just .09 inches hits the ball 8 yards higher with the driver. On a wood, a deeper c.g. means a higher trajectory. The farther back from the face a wood's c.g. is, the more the clubhead tries to turn under as the c.g. tries to line up with the shaft, resulting in a higher trajectory ball. For every .2 inches that the c.g. is moved back from the face, you get about 3 yards of extra height on your drives. Many pros fine tune the c.g. of the clubhead to control their ball's trajectory. Most of us just want to hit it straight.

Understanding how the club's center of gravity affects ball trajectory, helps in selecting the proper club. Unfortunately, clubs don't come with specs on where their center of gravity is. In general, cavity-backed irons carry their weight lower than blades. Look for clubs with heavy sole plates and thin toplines. Woods with shallow faces carry their weight low while deep-faced woods carry their weight higher. Smaller headed drivers carry their weight closer to the heel while oversize drivers carry their weight farther away. This is why many beginners tee off with their 3-wood over their driver. It is easier to turn the club over on the 3-wood, which is essential for not slicing the ball. Experimenting with moving the center of gravity around won't cure your bad golf swing, but it can sure make the ball fly like you intend it to.

WATCH OUT FOR THOSE OVERSIZE DRIVERS

Before you rush out to buy that potato-headed driver, be aware that if you have a slicing problem these clubs can sometimes make it worse. Many golfers think that because a clubhead has a bigger sweet spot, they can better control the dreaded slice as there is a better chance to hit the sweet spot. This is true to a certain degree, but slices are caused by striking the ball with an open clubface. You must close the clubface at impact to hit a straight shot. The closer the c.g. is to the heel of the club, the easier it is to close. This is the main reason that most golfers find it easier to draw the ball with a smaller clubhead such as a 3-wood. Many of the oversize heads carry their center of gravity more toward the toe making it harder to close. Be aware of this concept if you have problems with slicing or hooking. A suggestion here would be to experiment with adding lead tape to areas of your clubhead to redistribute the center of gravity.

GEAR EFFECT

Have you ever noticed that the face of your driver is not flat, but slightly convex? This is to help you straighten out your shot. If you hit the driver toward the toe, the club wants to twist out in a clockwise manner, or opposite the heel. The outwardly curved surface of the clubface helps to straighten out the shot by spinning the ball in the opposite rotation of the clubhead. The same theory applies if you hit the ball toward the heel. This phenomenon is called the *gear effect*.

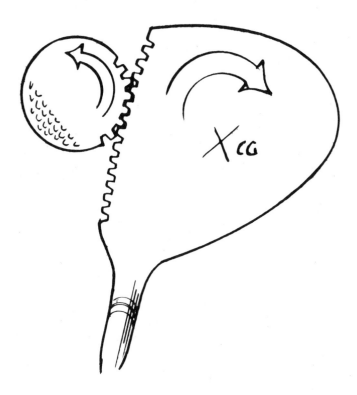

GEAR EFFECT

CHAPTER FOUR

GOLF EQUIPMENT
Outfitting the Player

While the golf swing is still the most critical aspect of improving your game, having the proper equipment can either enhance or inhibit this development. Most golfers are likely to buy clubs not really suited to their game. We are steered too much into buying clubs based on advertising. Just because Greg Norman plays with a certain brand of clubs does not mean you will be able to play like Greg if you buy the same clubs. The clubs he plays with are most likely not available to you anyway. Golf club manufacturers spend millions of dollars a year on advertising, and many of the higher priced clubs are priced that way to pay for the advertising. Higher costs do not necessarily mean you're getting a better club.

Golf, like any sport is best enjoyed if you have the proper equipment. With the many clubs available, it is a confusing ordeal to select the proper equipment that is best suited to your game. Also as important, are the accessories added to your ensemble to make your game more enjoyable. This chapter focuses on helping you find the right equipment for your game, and the enjoyment of your game.

READY FOR THE WEEKEND!

First we will look at what kinds of sets are available, then at the individual components of a golf club. It is important to understand how the different components change the playability. With this knowledge, you can better select clubs that are suited for your swing and temperament.

GOLF CLUB SETS

Nearly all the clubs available these days come in sets of irons; usually a 3-iron down to a pitching-wedge, and sets of woods; 1-driver, 3 and 5-fairway woods. The putter and sand wedge are usually not included and can be purchased separately.

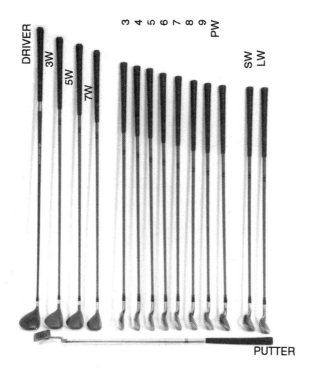

GOLF CLUB SET

Typical set plus additional 7-wood and loft-wedge.

To buy a complete set of clubs including the sand wedge and putter, you are looking at a minimum investment of $350 up to over $2,000. Be very careful about purchasing clubs much cheaper than the minimum as they are probably made of poor metals. You should always at least buy a stainless steel headed club. The old adage "you get what you pay for" is generally true. If you are a first-time golfer just starting out and do not have clubs, borrow some clubs from an understanding relative or friend to see if this is a sport you really want to get into. Many ranges and courses also have clubs you can rent. The trap some beginners fall into is to go out and buy an inexpensive "Starter Set", thinking that if they do not enjoy golfing, they will not have wasted much money. If you only play a couple of times a year, you will be much happier with a decent set of clubs over a cheap set. I would much rather see a first-timer buying a used set of clubs which can be picked up for a reasonable price.

When purchasing a new set, buy a set that you feel comfortable with that is within your price range. Swing every set in the store if you choose, and talk extensively with the salesperson. All good stores have knowledgeable sales staff and a place where you can hit balls. As your swing becomes established, you can select your clubs to better fit your game. If you are the type who has to have the best, and can afford it, try to get your swing established before you make your purchase. Many of the higher end clubs offer a wide range of shafts and heads that are available in the set. Your swing will determine what type of club, head and shaft will best suit your game. Let's examine the types of sets that are available.

THE STARTER SET

The so-called "Starter Set" usually costs under $150 and includes a couple of woods, four or five irons, and a putter. Whatever the sales person tells you, *I don't recommend purchasing these clubs*. These clubheads are usually cast of inferior metals and have little quality control. They usually come with an overly stiff shaft that inhibits most players, progress. You can hit shots with these clubs, but I think you will want to turn them into fishing weights as soon as your game starts to improve. You are better off buying a good set of used clubs that are available through newspaper ads, garages sales, or friends.

THE FULL SET

If you've decided to purchase new clubs, the first thing you need to do is find a good golf shop with knowledgeable staff. This golf shop should also have a place where you can test the clubs; this could be an actual outdoor range, or most likely an indoor testing area where you can hit into a net. Many of the better golf stores have computerized swing analyzers which can measure your swing speed as well as detect if you are hitting the ball with an open or closed clubface. *Always try out your clubs before purchasing them!* If you feel confident with the salesperson, ask him or her to look at your swing and let the salesperson suggest several clubs in your price range. If the clubs you prefer are out of your price range, just get the irons now and hold off on buying the woods. It is better to get a few clubs that *feel right* rather than all the clubs that only feel okay.

Typically irons are the basis for your complete set of clubs. On a well-matched set of irons, the swing weight should feel the same from the 3-iron down to the pitching-wedge. It is important that these clubs are matched to give you a consistent feel and the gradation of distance each club will achieve. Also, when purchasing the set, ask the salesperson if different shafts are available. Most manufacturers offer a choice between steel and graphite, but also look for different flex ratings. Most of the high-end manufacturers will give you a choice of several flex ratings.

Woods should be bought separately. There are so many different drivers on the market, you should not feel restricted to get one that matches your irons. Also, depending on the type of player you are and how aggressively you swing, you can get an array of head sizes, shaft stiffness, and loft angles that satisfy all your needs in a club. Many companies now offer titanium-headed drivers with an extra long shaft. With these clubs, most players can achieve greater distance off the tee, but the extra length of the shaft will magnify any problems in your swing. *You have to be confident about your driver!*

With fairway woods, you basically have the same choices as your driver. Most players carry a 3-wood and a 5-wood in their bag. Many players prefer to hit a 3-iron over a 5-wood. They will forego the extra wood for a different club; some add a 2-iron or 1-iron. Most find these clubs pretty tough to hit. You may also want to add a utility wood such as a 7-wood or a 9-wood. Many seniors and women prefer these clubs to long irons as they are usually easier to hit. *You can only carry 14 clubs in your bag when playing in tournaments.*

Next to the putter, the wedges are the most important clubs in your bag. These are the scoring clubs that are used on almost every shot inside 100 yards. This is where the professional player truly stands apart from the amateur. After you've played this game for some time, you will see that the players with a good short game are posting the best scores.

During a typical round of golf, sixty-three percent of your shots are going to be putts, pitches or chips. A good pitch close to the hole can take much of the pressure off your putting game.   Distance, ball trajectory and ball attitude (reaction of ball when it hits the green) are developed by the *feel* of the swing. When you watch the tour pros hit a pitch shot, notice that they take several quick repetitive practice swings; they are developing a *feel* for the shot. They might pick the ball up high and drop it onto the green softly, or pitch it low and let the ball roll up to the cup. It is important to have a wedge so that you develop control and feel for the shot. It is also important that your wedges match up to the rest of your set. Each wedge should get progressively shorter while the shafts get progressively softer. Shortening the shaft makes the swing plan more upright which makes it easier to hit a high soft shot. The shafts need to get softer so the club will retain its feel, even with a shorter shaft. In this way, your wedges will *feel* the same as your other irons.

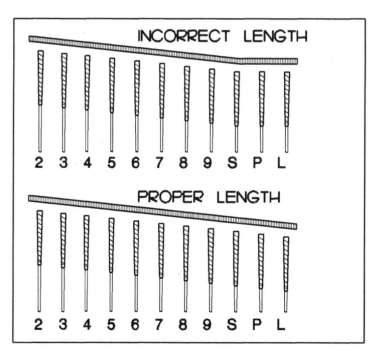

I hit almost all of my pitches inside 50 yards with a sand wedge. The sand wedge has a wide flange that allows you to bounce the club off the ground which, in turn tosses the golf ball high and soft. To hit a low bump and run, the heavy sole of the wedge allows the club to take a nice divot without impeding the swing. Confidence with this club pays big dividends in your game, so select a club that you feel confident swinging.

The putter is the most important and personal club in your bag. This is where you can make or break your game. When you go into a golf shop, they will probably carry a hundred different putters. They are too numerous to describe. Some have long shafts while some are short; some have large heads while others have the more traditional blade. The important thing is to test out many different putters and buy a putter that you are comfortable with from *day one.* It is a club that once you are happy with it, you will probably keep it for years.

CUSTOMIZED CLUBS

A set of clubs can be created to match a player's height, weight, build, swing-type and abilities. The only drawback with a complete custom set is that your favorite clubhead might not be available unless you buy that manufacturers set. But there are many quality clubheads offered to the custom clubfitter. A set of custom irons can range anywhere from $500 to around $1,400; custom woods go for around $120 to $300 each, which is comparable to some manufactured sets. Club customization can be accomplished in two ways:

1. A custom clubfitter can modify an existing set of clubs by reshafting the club (most important part of the club) and changing the grip or lie angle. In this way, you can retain

your favorite clubheads on a club suited to your swing.

2. Clubs can be assembled from scratch that are tailor made to your height, weight, swing, and stance. A good clubfitter will set you up with the right club in swing weight, shaft flex, club length, loft and lie, and your favorite grip. You can also pick out the brand of heads that your clubs are fitted with. You can also designate which irons, wedges and woods you will carry in this set. If you ever break a club, you can simply call the clubfitter and he will make you up a new club. This will always be your best set, unless you change your swing.

When shopping for a clubmaker, don't overlook the small shops. Most have low overhead and offer good pricing on quality clubs. The biggest change in recent years has been the introduction of *knockoffs*. Knockoffs are clubs similar to brandname clubs; not copies. A person can go to jail for manufacturing a counterfeit club, but only has to pay a civil fine for manufacturing a knockoff. In 1995, an estimated $40 million worth of golf components were imported into the U.S. from the far east alone. When you visit a custom golf shop, you'll see clubs that look like; Callaway Big Berthas, Taylor Made Burner Bubbles, Lynx Black Cat Irons and so forth. Many have the same markings and logos, but only the names are different. If the logo and shape of the club matches the real club, this is probably a counterfeit. If the club is similar in logo and shape, this club is a knockoff. There is a fine line between knockoff and counterfeit; most reputable shops will stay away from the counterfeit clubs. These clubs can be up to seventy-five percent less than the real ones. A set of Callaway Big Bertha irons can cost around $2,000 dollars whereas as the Big Brother irons (knockoff) will cost around $500 dollars. But buyer beware—you generally get what you pay for. If you are considering knockoff clubs, try to play with the set you are interested in. The clubmaker will usually have a set for demo. Some knockoffs are good while others are junk. I've played with a set of Taylor Made Burner Bubbles, and a set of Callaway Big Berthas. I've also played with the knockoff versions of these clubs. I couldn't tell much of a difference. But I've also tried some other knockoffs that were complete junk. Try every club you are considering. If you decide to buy a knockoff, be careful because you might get just what you paid for. If you buy the *original,* you at least know you are getting a quality product backed by the company.

Let's examine the pieces that make up the clubs. With the knowledge gained here, you will better be able to select the club or clubs that are right for you.

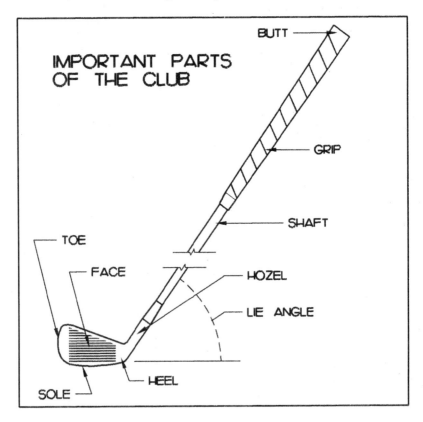

WOOD CLUBHEADS

Most modern woods are cast from stainless steel. With a hollow center, the cavity is usually filled with foam to reduce impact noise. Metal woods are usually perimeter-weighted which helps most amateurs hit the ball with more power. This design puts more mass on the toe and heel which helps with off-center hits. By spreading the clubhead's weight out, you can still achieve good distance with an off-centered hit. These metal woods also carry their center of gravity lower than the old traditional woods; it means they will hit a higher ball. Recently, several manufacturers introduced a titanium headed driver that has a bigger sweet spot. The strength and lightness of titanium allows the clubhead to be larger, but also carries a larger price tag.

Attention all slicers! If you think you are going to get rid of your slice by purchasing an oversize driver, refer to the page 43 on golf physics.

You also get a wide choice of loft angles on the drivers, ranging from an 8-degree driver for the low handicapper seeking maximum distance to a 12-degree driver for the player who has trouble getting the ball up in the air.

For the traditionalists, real *woods* are available. They are usually made of persimmon and offer the skilled golfer a certain degree of craftsmanship. Many golfers claim that the real woods offer better feel and control than the metal wood. You have to hit these clubs fairly dead center or you're bound to get an unsatisfactory result.

IRON CLUBHEADS

As mentioned before, avoid *cast alloy* clubheads. They are not suited for an aggressive swing and can crack. They also lack the quality controls used on the better clubs, and are seldom used in other than low-end sets. At minimum, look for stainless steel heads. Some manufacturers now offer titanium heads which are a lighter weight, but these carry a high price tag.

There are still a small percentage of golfers who prefer the forged irons. Many pros play forged irons because these clubs offers great control and feel. But pros hit their clubs dead center and seldom mishit. Most amateurs cannot strike the ball with the same power or consistency of a pro and need a club that is much more forgiving. Thus, the best clubs for many amateurs are the cavity-backed irons. Most of the clubs in a golf store will be this type.

Most of these irons are made of stainless steel. These clubs are perimeter-weighted which straightens and adds distance to off-center hits. These clubs also carry their weight lower, which causes the ball to fly higher. Generally, clubheads for seniors and women carry a lower center of gravity that helps hit the ball high to attain distance. If you make an aggressive swing, you might want a club with a higher center of gravity that allows you to hit that boring shot.

Also, look at the hozels of the clubs you are considering. The more the hozel is offset from the shaft, the more the clubhead will straighten out the shot. While this is great to help the high-handicapper straighten out his or her shots, it is restrictive to the low handicapper who desires to shape their shots.

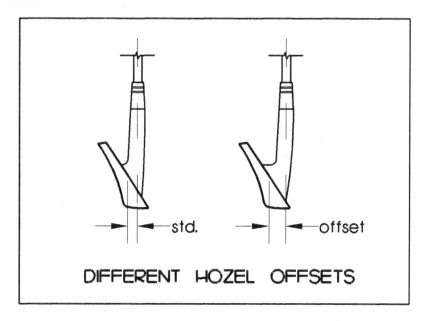

DIFFERENT HOZEL OFFSETS

Wedges are available in lofts of 50-degrees to over 60-degrees. The wedges in your bag are your scoring clubs. These clubs are available in a wide range of lofts and different sole designs with varying bounces. The term *bounce* refers to the design of the sole which determines how it reacts to different surfaces of dirt, grass or sand. You want these clubs to bounce off the surface you are striking and not dig in. This allows the club to slide under the ball pitching it high in the air. A pitching wedge will generally be included with your set of irons, but the sand wedge and optional loft wedge will be purchased separately. Before you run out and buy the first sand wedge you see, examine the following illustrations. They will help you select a wedge for your game and the courses you play.

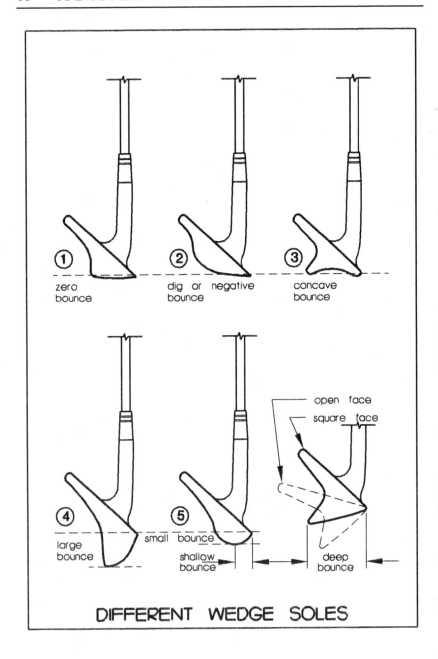

DIFFERENT WEDGE SOLES

The different wedge designs are good for the following conditions and lies:

1. Square face: Good for hardpan and tight fairways
   Open face: Fairways, hard or wet sand

2. Square face: Planting vegetables
   Open face: Hardpan dirt and sand

3. Square face: Tight fairways and moist sand
   Open face: Normal rough, soft/fine sand

4. Square face: Normal to deep rough
   Open face: Deep rough and soft/fine sand

5. Square face: Fairways, and first cut of rough
   Open face: Light rough, firm moist sand

Try to purchase a wedge with the sole design that is suited for the conditions you play under most often. Depending on the courses you play and the area in which you live, you should experiment with different wedge shapes to determine which style plays the best.

CLUB SHAFTS

The shaft of the club is most likely the most important and overlooked component of the club. *It is the engine that powers the car!* The shaft's job is to return the clubhead squarely to the ball during the swing. If the shaft is not suited to your swing, you will lose distance, direction and control.

Shafts are generally made of two different materials, steel or graphite. Steel shafts are usually stiffer than graphite, which requires a more aggressive swing. Steel may offer better control and feel for a low-handicap player who likes to get maximum feedback from the clubhead. The disadvantage is that steel transmits the shock of an off-center hit. A graphite shaft is generally easier to swing due to its light weight and offers more distance for a player with a slower clubhead speed. As development of graphite or composite shafts moves forward, more and more low-handicap players will switch over. Years ago on the pro tour, almost everyone used steel. In recent years, many have switched to graphite for their drivers. On a recent trip to AT&T's Pebble Beach tournament, I observed many pros playing full graphite sets. With the advances in the development of the graphite shaft, the new shafts offer the stiffness of steel, but with the forgiving qualities of graphite. A word of warning: *Do not buy cheap graphite.* When you look at a club fitted with a graphite shaft, grab the clubhead in one hand and the grip in the other; then twist. If you can twist this club back and forth, there is no way this clubface is ever going to square at impact. Buying cheap-graphite shafted clubs is a waste of money.

If you took a high speed film of the golf swing, you would see that the shaft bends and straightens during the swing. During the downswing, the clubhead lags slightly behind bending or *loading* the shaft. This loading of the shaft is building power to be released through the ball. As the clubhead approaches the ball, the shaft *unloads* or straightens out as the clubhead strikes the ball. Sometimes the clubhead will move ahead of the shaft at impact; this is okay as long as the clubhead is still accelerating. This whipping of the shaft kicks the golf ball producing more power in the shot.

If the shaft is too flexible for your swing, it will load early in your swing and unload early, before the clubhead impacts the ball.   The clubhead will already be decelerating when it contacts the ball with a closed face thus producing a weak shot to the left.

TOO FLEXIBLE

If the shaft is too stiff, the shaft will not load properly and will never reach maximum speed. The clubhead will contact the ball with an open face and the ball will fly low and weakly to the right.

TOO STIFF

When the shaft is proper to your swing, it will unload just before impact. The loaded-up shaft springs back so that the clubhead contacts the ball with the maximum amount of energy.

PROPER FLEX

Shafts are also available with different kick points; a high kick point will produce a lower shot. A low kick point will produce a higher shot. Shafts also have a natural spine. As the shaft bends, the stiffest side of the shaft will naturally turn toward the outside radius of the bend. Properly positioned, the spine should face the target. The shaft will whip back and forth parallel with the spine.

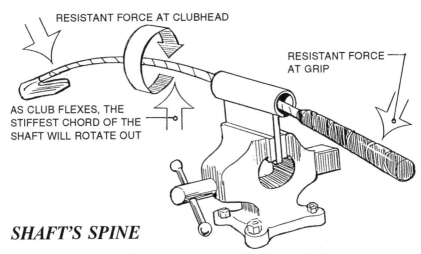

RESISTANT FORCE AT CLUBHEAD

RESISTANT FORCE AT GRIP

AS CLUB FLEXES, THE STIFFEST CHORD OF THE SHAFT WILL ROTATE OUT

SHAFT'S SPINE

Most amateurs swing the clubhead between 75 and 95 miles per hour. A regular or firm shaft would be best choice. Most seniors and women players swing slower and will require a softer flex shaft. Touring pros such as Greg Norman or Ernie Els swing the clubhead at up to 125 miles per hour. They require a stiff shaft or tour shaft. The big mistake many amateurs make is thinking they generate tremendous clubhead speed, just because they swing hard. They go out and get a shaft that is too stiff and wonder why they are hitting the ball short, or blocking many shots.

The key to generating clubhead speed and power is not through effort, but through form. This is discussed later in the book in the *Power Golf Chapter*. Just be aware of your swing speed to help you in selecting the proper shaft.

GRIPS

There's not much to say here. The important thing is to select a grip that is comfortable and of proper size. If you go the customization route, then you can select any grip that is available. If you go with a manufactured set, your choices may be limited. The key is to select a grip that is comfortable and feels right in your hands.

To determine the correct grip size, pick up a club with your left hand (right hand for lefties). If your middle two fingers wrap around the club and your fingertips touch the fleshy part of your palm, the grip is the correct size. If your fingertips cannot touch your hand, the grip is too big. This can restrict the cupping of your wrists which is so important in developing power. If your fingertips dig into your hand, the grip is too small. This can cause the clubhead to rotate on impact.

PUTTERS

Putters are a personal preference. You can buy putters in every form imaginable. The important things to look for when purchasing your putter are:

1. It feels good in your hands.

2. The putter's sole lies flat on the ground in your stance.

The most important thing you can do with any putter is to find the sweet spot. The only way to get consistency in your putting is to hit the ball on the sweet spot every time. To find the sweet spot, hold the putter grip between two fingers. Do not hold the putter vertically; angle it as if you were putting. Take a metal, pointed object such as a key and tap along the face of the putter until you feel the sweet spot. This is the spot that swings the club back and forth with no rotation of the face or wobble to the club.   It is also the spot that produces minimum vibration.   When you find it, mark it on top of the putter.   Don't trust the marks that come on the putter.   Hitting the ball on the sweet spot, will give you consistent feedback, which is the key to putting success.

PUTTERS

GOLF BALLS

When I first started playing, I bought the assorted balls in a bag; a dozen balls for six dollars. In those days, I would lose a half dozen-balls in a single round. Once your game gets to where you're playing with one or two balls, you should consider what type of ball will aid your game. It used to be that two-piece balls were made for distance and three-piece balls were made for control. Two-piece balls usually had a highly elastic and durable cover (Surlyn) over a solid core. Three-piece balls usually had a soft balata cover over a liquid core wrapped by rubber bands or threads. With the changes in cover and core materials, more manufacturers are making combination distance/control balls and high-spin two-piece balls. Balls can also be found with different trajectory designs; high-trajectory balls for players who need to hit a higher ball for distance, regular-trajectory balls for most players; low-trajectory or tour-trajectory for players who do not have a problem getting the ball in the air and are seeking maximum distance. There are three types of balls on the market:

1. *Low-spin ball:* This is usually a two-piece ball made for maximum distance and minimal curvature off the tee. This is the anti-slice/anti-hook ball that helps most high-handicappers who are looking for distance and need help staying in the fairway. The Surlyn cover is resistant to cutting and scuffing which makes this a very durable ball; the drawback is less distance control and stopping power around the greens.

2. *Compromise ball:* This ball is for the player who needs a little more control around the greens while still needing a little help off the tee. It won't be as long as a low-spin ball, but it does offer more spin which will help the ball stop on a green. Most compromise balls have a durable cover made of Surlyn that is resistant to cuts and scuffs. This is a good ball for middle handicappers who are comfortable in keeping their balls in the fairways.

3. *High-spin ball:* This is generally a three-piece ball that offers maximum control in distance and trajectory. The cover is usually a soft material giving superior feel on and around the green. Most low-handicappers use this type of ball because it gives them the ability to shape their

shots (left-to-right or right-to-left). Due to the soft cover, these balls will produce a lot of back-spin with medium to short irons which is essential in controlling the amount of roll a ball has landing on a green. There are drawbacks with these balls: the soft cover is easy to cut so an off center hit could cut the ball; since the balls spin much faster than the distance balls, any slice or hook that you hit with the distance balls could turn into a big banana-slice or duck-hook. All mistakes are magnified with a high-spin ball.

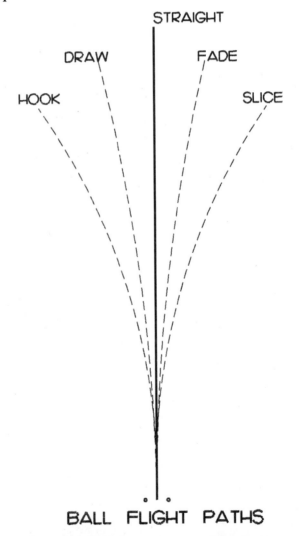

BALL FLIGHT PATHS

ACCESSORY EQUIPMENT

There is an endless array of accessories that you can buy to aid your game. Some are essential and everyone should carry them. Some are extraneous and are not necessary to play, but can add comfort and enjoyment to your game.

ESSENTIAL EQUIPMENT:

1. *Golf shoes:* It is hard to make a consistent swing when you are slipping and sliding all over the wet grass as you try to kill the ball. Nothing helps your confidence more than a good pair of golf shoes. You can find shoes in many styles and shapes, but make sure they are comfortable. Remember, you will walk over 5 miles during a round of golf. Also try to get waterproof shoes if possible. Even during the summer, you are bound to get into areas of standing water. Be sure to check your spikes as they wear down very fast walking over parking lots. Change them periodically before they get so worn down that you can never remove them. *Note: When installing spikes, put vaseline on the threads; it will make them much easier to remove.*

2. *Glove:* With the arrival of new grip materials, the glove is not as important as it used to be. But it does help in keeping your hand on the club, especially under damp conditions. When the glove starts to become stiff or worn, replace it. Don't wait until it wears completely through because it will then bunch up on your hand.

3. *Ball mark fixer:* This is a very important tool that all golfers should carry. There is nothing worse than golfers who do not fix their ball marks. Lots of golfers use golf tees, but they don't work properly for repairing ball

marks. Learn how to use this tool and always fix your ball marks left on the green, then fix someone else's.

4. *Golf towel:* Be sure to carry a towel for wiping off your hands, your ball, and your clubs. If you want a towel to wipe off your face on a hot day, carry an additional towel.

5. *Water:* Carry a bottle of drinking water in your golf bag. Many courses are inadequate with drinking fountains or available water stations. It is very important not to allow yourself to get dehydrated so always carry water.

6. *Food:* You may find yourself rushing off to the golf course barely making tee times, never having time for a proper meal. Your body will wear down and definitely lets you know when it needs some nourishment. Slip a couple of candy bars or some fruit into your bag instead of all those beers. You can always get beer after you play.

7. *Sunscreen:* With all the dangers of skin cancer you need to protect yourself. Make sure you get a waterproof sunscreen, spf 15 or better. Pay particular attention to those areas behind the neck and ears as they are subject to severe burns. If you are balding, consider a hat.

8. *Golf tees:* Be sure your bag is stocked with tees, unless you plan to hit everything off the ground.

9. *Insect repellant:* Golf courses need water, and water breeds mosquitoes. Keep a small bottle of insect repellant in your bag.

EXTRANEOUS EQUIPMENT

1. *Ball retriever:* If you play courses that have water hazards, you may want to invest in a ball retriever. This will pay for itself by enabling you to retrieve all the balls that you or the group in front of you hit into the water.

2. *Pull cart:* I like to walk around a course because it not only gives me a better perspective on the course, but it is good exercise. A pull cart is a good alternative to carrying your bag. Many players will not use these because it is not the *man's way* to walk a course; I've heard people call it an *old lady cart.* But if you have to walk over five miles up and down hills, in the heat of the day over a four hour period, not having to lug a bag over your *now* sloping shoulders, can keep you fresher throughout the round.

3. *Band-Aids:* If you have problems with blisters on your hands or feet, carry a small pack of Band-Aids in your bag.

4. *First-Aid Kit:* A small first-aid kit might come in handy for minor cuts and scrapes, especially if you go off into the bushes to look for your ball.

5. *Felt-tip permanent marker:* You can do this at home, but marking your balls might keep others from accidentally playing your ball on the course.

6. *Golf hat:* Golf hats are a great idea in very sunny climates. They are very porous to allow air to flow through them, but they also do a good job blocking out much of the sun from your neck and face. They can also shade your eyes and absorb some sweat off your brow.

7. *Golf attire:* It is always a good idea to find out if the course you are playing has a dress code. Many courses will make you wear a collared shirt and not allow blue jeans. If you wear shorts, they have to be a golf type short, not cutoffs. While a tank top might be comfortable on a beach, it is not appropriate in a restaurant or on a golf course. Use your best judgement.

8. *Foul-weather gear:* Dress appropriately if you are going to play in inclement weather.   Most golf shops carry waterproof shells that work well to keep your body shielded from wind and moisture. Make sure you try everything on to verify that the clothes you purchase will allow you to make an uninhibited golf swing.

9. *Wire brush:* A small wire brush is a useful tool for cleaning the grooves on your clubs. Keeping the grooves clean will help put spin on the ball which is important to hold greens.

10. *Sunglasses:* These not only provide protection and shading for your eyes on sunny days, but you will look *cool* strutting up to the clubhouse.

Like any sport you participate in, proper equipment and physical preparation goes a long way in making the game more fun and less frustrating. A little research in selecting the right equipment does wonders for your confidence as you learn to play golf.

CHAPTER FIVE

THE GOLF SWING
A Natural Approach

If no one has developed the better mousetrap yet, they are probably too busy reinventing the golf swing. There have been more books and articles written, more gadgets invented, and more instruction provided on the golf swing. This is a multimillion dollar a year industry because as long as there are golfers playing, there are golfers looking for a way to perfect their swings. It seems that every golfer has his or her own opinion on the proper technique. This is why many high handicappers get so confused on just what to do. Many just get bogged down with the mechanics of the swing. Thinking about the swing too much will do more harm than good.

In an effort to obtain that perfect swing, golfers will try just about anything. They will buy anything to help improve their swings, videotapes, books, magazines. Many golfers purchase swing-training-aids; clubs that hinge, straps that keep your hands together, tubes that keep your arm straight, braces that keep your legs from collapsing, bells that ring when you swing inside-out, grips that chirp when you squeeze too hard, contraptions that strap on to your wrist to ensure you release them, and so forth. There's even a machine that measures your swing speed and tempo.

DUFFER'S NEW GOLF SWING!

With all the inventions, theories, and techniques surrounding the golf swing, it's no wonder why it is a source of frustration for the beginner. Golfers make the golf swing much harder than it really is. If they would just learn to relax, swing nice and easy, they will achieve better results.

A good swing is a natural swing! The simpler you make your swing, the more consistent your swing will be. You cannot make confident shots if your swing has no consistency.

A natural swing is a rhythmical swing! When you free your body of tension and allow your natural movements to guide the swing, your arms and hands will be relaxed allowing the club to do what it was designed to do—hit the ball high and straight.

A rhythmical swing is a powerful swing! By letting your body find it's own rhythm, you can let the bigger muscles take over. The small muscles go along for the ride. This will whip the clubhead through at maximum speed with little speed-robbing tension.

KUNG FU GOLF

Martial arts are based on the *natural movements* of different animals. I began studying martial arts in 1976. I remember my first day in class, watching the instructor move with such grace and power; he seemed to flow effortlessly to each position. I remember my first lesson; I felt unbalanced, awkward and expended a lot of energy trying to duplicate those moves. Most of my early lessons were limited to the repeated drilling of basic blocks, stances, basic kicks, and punches. We started every lesson with repeated drilling of basics. It became frustrating for me because I was taking lessons to learn how to fight. My instructors would not let me spar anyone until I earned my green belt. To earn that green belt, I had to go through four other belts (white, orange, purple, and blue). I thought "it would take me at least a year and I wanted to learn how to fight immediately!" After I got thumped by a little guy wearing a purple belt, I became more humble. As I progressed through each degree of the different belts, it became clear to me why I was not allowed to spar; it was because I wasn't ready.

I later learned that each belt taught a different discipline. Each discipline built upon the previous one like building blocks for a building. I also learned that most of these colored belts are an American invention. In the Orient, students go from white to green to brown and then to black. In the U.S. it takes going through twenty-four levels over six colored belts, before reaching black. There seems to be a need for constant reinforcement. It seems we, as Americans, do not possess the infinite patience of the Asian.

I liken this process to learning how to play golf. When performed by a professional, golf is a martial art. The tour pro is a black belt; he or she performs the craft with skill, making the difficult look effortless. Pros were not born that way, their skills were developed over years of training. Anyone can pick up a set of clubs and play a round of golf with little or no instruction. It may take a dozen golf balls, and the better part of a day to complete the round, but they will have played. That's fine if you're out to have fun, but if you are competitive and seek improvement in your game, proper preparation is the key. The main reason so many amateurs develop bad habits they fight their whole life is because they have never received proper instruction. You seek improvement. Why else would you be reading this book? So let's put that white belt back on and start with the basics.

First we will view the golf swing as a karate move. Karate techniques are a sequence of stances. The movements between each stance are flowing and not disruptive. Each stance has a purpose in the technique, each movement is performed with minimal energies.   There are no wasted motions moving from stance to stance, nor any muscles working against one another. The golf swing is a sequence of stances; how you get to each stance is not that important, as long as each stance is realized and the timing between each one is flowing.

This is where most amateurs get bogged down and develop problems in their swings. They have been told so many things about the mechanics of the golf swing, they tend to think about it too technically. This technical information gets them all tangled up which prevents a natural and flowing swing. How many times have you stepped up to the first tee with a hundred different things going through your head?   How many times have you tried to change your swing while playing a round of golf?

By starting with a white belt and building your swing through the proper sequence, you will develop a natural swing that will prepare you to compete on the golf course.

WHITE BELT

The white belt teaches preparation.   Everyone taking karate lessons receives a white belt; it comes with the uniform and you *gotta hold up your pants*.   As a white belt, physical conditioning is stressed. It includes exercise and stretching. The rank of white belt in golf is to obtain the proper equipment, and prepare yourself physically.

ORANGE BELT

The orange belt teaches basics.   Here you learn the basic stances, blocks, punches and kicks.   The fundamentals are continually drilled until they become automatic. As an orange belt in golf, you learn basic techniques: the full swing, the short game, and how to play out of sand traps. You practice basic shotmaking and the distance each club carries the ball. Swing fundamentals are practiced until they become ingrained. A good foundation of fundamentals is essential to progress in the game.

PURPLE BELT

The purple belt teaches power and balance. Here you learn how to develop power from your lower body. By using your legs and hips, you learn to develop tremendous power in your punches. You learn that a solid foundation will keep you balanced. In your golf swing, you learn to use your lower body to develop power. The largest muscles in your body are located in the lower half. A strong foundation provides the basis for a powerful swing while keeping the twisting body in balance.

BLUE BELT

The blue belt teaches speed. Here you learn by freeing your body from excess tension; your strikes will be delivered with incredible speed and accuracy. By allowing the body to relax, muscles do not compete against one another; they work together to obtain the objective—a crushing blow. By freeing your body from tension, you allow your natural movements to coil and release during the swing. By not swinging the clubs with your arms, the arms will follow the body rotation allowing the club to stay on plane. The leverage created by the unhinging of the arms and wrists creates tremendous power. This allows the club to whip through the striking zone building tremendous clubhead speed.

GREEN BELT

The green belt teaches range of motion. Now you are ready to spar; the techniques learned from the other belts should be a part of you and be as natural as walking. Any adjustments to your techniques at this point are minor. You no longer have to concentrate on the movements, but devote your full attention to your opponent. In golf, now is the time to concentrate on your target. You shouldn't be caught up with techniques on how you reach it. You are no longer reinventing your golf swing on the tee. Your swing should be ingrained, so your full attention can be focused on the target. You have attained confidence in your golf swing.

BROWN BELT

The brown belt teaches advanced techniques. Here you learn how to fight multiple opponents with advanced techniques, how to use weapons, and how to handle difficult situations. When the rank of brown belt is obtained, you move with total confidence in your technique. In golf, you are utilizing advanced techniques: how to shape shots, how to draw and fade the ball, how to handle different trouble shots. Your game goes to a new level, your handicap is reaching single digits, and you're considered an advanced player. When the golfer achieves his or her brown belt, he can adjust his game to the course and conditions to play it aggressively.

BLACK BELT

You are now an expert. You have conquered all the basics and the advanced techniques. You are now concentrating on mastering the different animals and developing your own techniques and style. Nobody messes with you anymore. In golf, you are a *Player*. Par golf is routine work for you as you seek to shoot under par. You are looking for competition and travel to many tournaments. Your friends will not compete against you unless you give them a dozen strokes. You are a complete player!

RED BELT

You are now a teacher. Now that you have an understanding of the different levels of development, let's go back to the beginning. In my seven years as an instructor of martial arts, I have seen every type of student imaginable: tall, short, skinny, fat, humble, cocky, quiet, loud—every different size and shape, along with assorted dispositions. But they all had one thing in common; they were all interested in karate. Martial arts training has a very specific agenda on how students are instructed. Students must learn basics before moving on to more advanced techniques. Advanced techniques are derived from basic techniques, only the timing changes. Each lesson has a specific goal and builds a foundation on which later lessons will be applied. Basic stances and positions are the foundation for all martial arts techniques. Without this solid foundation to build on, all techniques afterward lose effectiveness since too much energy is channeled to maintain the foundation and not the technique.

In golf, we have the same scenario. We all come in varying sizes and shapes, and seek ways to improve our game. I often see people at the range or on the course standing in the most unusual positions as they get ready to hit the ball. I know that if they don't hurt themselves swinging, they are going to hit a bad shot. Most of these players developed their stances over the years through trial and error. Through sheer will they've found a stance that occasionally lets them hit the ball straight. They're working so hard just to keep the ball in the fairway;

all of their concentration is focused on hitting the ball. They forget the objective, the target!

The lesson here is that if you want to improve your game, you need a *solid foundation* to build upon. Don't develop a stance that leaves you unbalanced. You cannot make a good golf swing without a solid, well-balanced stance. Take some time to build your swing; check your stance, and practice your techniques. Earn that orange belt before worrying about the purple.

SETUP POSITION—WELL-BALANCED

THE GOLF SWING

Balance is the most important element in the martial arts. A good fighting stance is one where you're balanced and ready to strike or defend. Beginning fighters flail and kick at their opponents only to lose accuracy and balance. They expend a tremendous amount of energy with their feudal techniques. To regain control, the fighter has to calm down, get back his timing, re-establish his rhythm, conserve his energy, and maintain his balance. In golf the same theories apply; you must establish rhythm and timing to maintain your balance. Balance is developed from the setup position—through to the finish position.

FINISH POSITION—WELL-BALANCED

I've seen golfers swing so hard they lose their balance or twist out of their stance. In an effort to hit the ball a long way, most amateurs swing too hard. Swinging hard not only creates tension in your muscles, but causes you to lose your balance.

TRYING TO KILL THE BALL!

To obtain rhythm and balance in karate, you learn to perform a sequence of movements called *katas*. A kata incorporates a series of imaginary opponents that the student attacks and defends himself from. Some katas require over one hundred different techniques, but are performed as one continual movement. They require *smooth tempo, timing, and rhythm* to stay in balance. The golf swing is similar to a kata in that it has several positions, but is performed as one continual movement. It also requires *smooth tempo, timing and rhythm* to stay in balance.

When your game starts getting bad, you must:

- *Calm yourself*

- *Get back to the basics*

- *Re-establish your rhythm*

- *Clear your head.*

The golf swing has many parts. The critical positions of the swing are the *setup, position at the top, Point A, and the finish position.*

a.   *Setup:* Sets the tone for the whole swing and is the base for keeping your balance.

b.   *Position at the top:* Sets up the actual striking of the ball. It's not that important how you get here, but this position must be correct to allow for a good downswing.

c.   *Point A:* Hitting Point A on the downswing guarantees that the club is on the proper plane. Missing point A will cause varying and inconsistent results.

d.   *Finish position:* A good finish is hard to fake. If everything before goes okay, the body should end here naturally.

THE SETUP POSITION

A good swing begins with a good setup. You can't make a good golf swing without a solid setup. Jack Nicklaus once said that the main reason many amateur players fail to attain their full playing potential is that they do not pay enough attention to their *statics.* Eighty percent of good shotmaking happens before the club even moves. When the body is properly balanced and postured, it allows the swing to freely rotate around the body. This is why it is so important to get proper instruction. Many high-handicappers make adjustments during their swings in an effort to hit the ball straight. This is mainly because their setups are so bad. We want to build the swing step by step by looking at the individual parts. The setup begins with a good grip, stance, and ball position.

The setup is much more than a physical pose, it is also a mental state of being. When you are standing over the ball, it is not the time to be analyzing your swing. All your thinking should be done behind the ball. By the time you step up to the ball, hitting the ball is the only task at hand. Later in the book, we cover swing thoughts and a pre-shot routine which is essential for adding consistency to your game. When you step up to the ball, don't let your mind wander; it's like in the Nike commercial, *just do it!*

Before movements can take place, there must be a change of muscular tension on both sides of the joints to be moved. The effectiveness of this muscular teamwork is one of the factors which determine limits of speed, endurance, power, agility and accuracy in all athletic performances. [3]

3: Bruce Lee, <u>Tao of Jeet Kune Do</u> (Ohara Publications, Copyright 1975)

THE GRIP

The grip largely determines where the clubface is aimed at impact. First understand that the only parts of your body touching the club are your hands. It is very important that your grip be in a natural position as the body will always try to return to its natural position. Removing tension from the arms lets the club swing freely which allows the club and hands to turn over at impact. This is key to making a good shot. To relieve tension in the arms, the grip must be *firm but relaxed*. The club has to be held firmly enough to keep it from flopping around and twisting in your hands, but loose enough to let the arms and hands work with the natural movements of the swing.

To find the correct grip:

1.   Simply stand erect with a club (preferably a driver) resting against your beltline. Make sure that the sole or bottom of the club is flat on the ground.

2.   Lean forward and let your arms hang down naturally. You should have enough room between your body and your grip to allow the club to pass cleanly through. *Continue to let your arms hang naturally even after gripping the club. Do not lift your left arm and angle it even with the club shaft. This prevents your arms from hanging down naturally.*

3.   Without turning or twisting, bring your hands in toward the club and wrap them around the club.

4.   Let the club settle naturally into your left hand. If your arms are still hanging down, the club will lay across the base of your fingers. Now let your left thumb press the

top-right side of the grip. The "V" formed by your thumb and forefinger should be pointing toward your right ear.

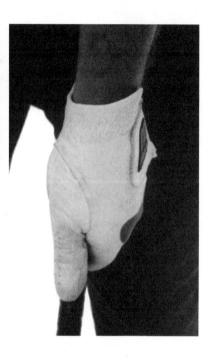 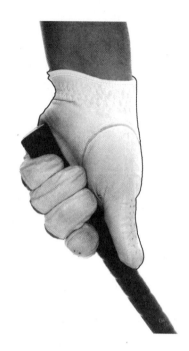

Traditional teaching tells us to hold the club in the palm of the left hand between the fleshy pads with the thumb on top. I found this to be physically impossible without lifting the shaft up parallel to the arm. If you grip the club in this manner, your arms extend only to reach the ball. With extended arms, you will produce the dreaded baseball swing which usually translates to a weak fade or a duck hook.

5. Let your right hand overlap the left hand. The pinky of your right hand either interlocks or overlaps the forefinger and middle fingers of your left hand. The club should lay across the base of the fingers of the right hand. The left thumb should fit between the fleshy pads of the right hand. Do not place the right thumb on top of the

club, wrap it over to the left. The "V" formed by your right hand points to your right shoulder. Having both hands on the club allows better control and feel of the club while promoting a strong release. This grip allows the clubface to close like it should promoting a powerful draw (ball with topspin).

6. If everything is in order, the back of your left hand should be square to the target, and the right just the opposite. The key here is that the hands must feel secure and comfortable on the club. If you feel that the hands are in

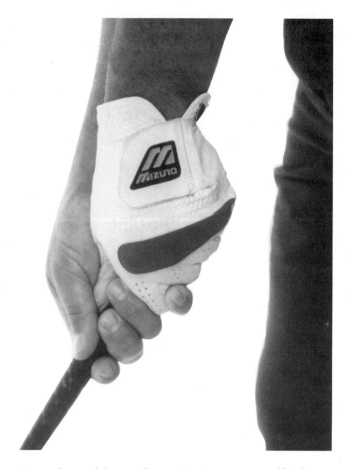

an awkward position, then start over until they are comfortable. *Remember, firm, but relaxed grip pressure.* This is a very *neutral and natural grip* that delivers the clubface to the ball squarely and consistently. A neutral grip ensures that both hands are released together producing optimum power. Any adjustments made to the grip to suit your individual needs should be very minor.

Make sure that the left arm is above the right when viewed from behind the ball. This will ensure the proper inside take-away.

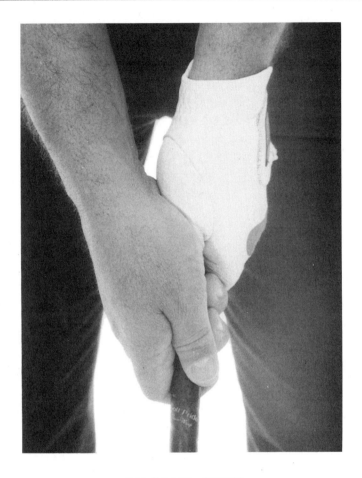

PROPER GRIP

A word of caution: Be careful about overcompensating your grip for a bad swing. Have you ever been told by someone to get rid of your slice by rotating your hands into a stronger grip? This is a band-aid repair to a problem in your swing. Many beginners play with the back of their left hand facing the sky, and the right hand facing the ground. This is a very strong grip used in an effort to get rid of that big banana slice. This is where two wrongs make a half-right. A closed clubface caused by a strong grip, and an out-to-in swing, will give you one of those cartoon shots that starts low and to the left and then makes a big turn to the right. If you are lucky, the ball will stay in the fairway.

THE STANCE

The stance is the foundation for a good swing and affects your swing more than anything else. There are many different opinions on what makes a good stance; the weight distribution between your right and left side, the width of your stance, placement of the ball in relation to your stance, which way your toes point, how much you bend over the ball, etc.? A good stance is one that is comfortable; one that allows you to swing through the ball; one that keeps you balanced; one that allows each club to work with your individual swing. Most tour players stand fairly erect and share a wide stance. Amateurs hold stances and postures that make many sure candidates for chiropractic care. You have to be comfortable when making a swing. When your body is not comfortable, it is trying to tell you something. It's saying that this posture you're forcing on it is *unnatural.*   If we analyze each component of the stance, we can establish one that works best for you.

The first thing every golfer wonders is how wide he or she should stand. The answer is simple. *You stand wide enough to keep from sliding and stay in balance, but narrow enough to allow your hips to properly rotate through until they are square to your target.* Typically, a wider stance for a beginner is better because it promotes a hip turn rather than a slide. But too wide a stance keeps your knees from flexing which prevents your hips from properly turning. This restriction of the hips also restricts the shoulder turn which reduces power. A good starting point is to begin with your heels about shoulder width apart. Use a slightly wider stance for the driver. This is to ensure that any sliding of the hips is minimized and resistance is allowed to build as the body coils.

The right foot should point straight ahead, and the left foot should point about 15 to 20 degrees to the left. Having the right foot squared gives you a solid leg with which to brace yourself. Having the left foot angled out helps the hips to turn square to the target. Your weight should be 50/50, more on the balls of your feet, not on your toes or heels. Don't worry about shifting your weight; it happens automatically with your natural swing movements. Be careful not to point your right foot to the right or out. This pigeon-toed stance inhibits the hip rotation and also disrupts your balance, and you will probably have to pick up your right foot to complete the swing.

Now flex your knees slightly, and tilt your body forward about 20 to 30 degrees, keeping your head up. This ensures a straight back. You should feel your weight in the balls of your feet. I detest the saying, "bend your knees" because most high-handicappers bend over too much. If you bend over too much, it is hard to deliver the club on plane. If you stand too straight, you lose power generated by your legs and hips. *You should feel as though you are about to sit on a bar stool.* By keeping your knees flexed and your head up, your spine stays straight to ensure a still or quiet lower body. When your spine is straight, your swing remains still. Remember the quiet lower body from golf physics? This enables your body to have maximum rotation and allows you to swing through the ball on an inside-out plane. With your body tilted properly and your head up, you can let your arms hang down and grip the club. The shaft of the club should be pointing to the inside of your left thigh, with your right shoulder and right knee lining up just inside the ball of your right foot.

Don't try to level your shoulders! I've had people tell me that
the shoulders need to be level. This is physically impossible
if you are properly setup. When your right hand is under your
left hand, it is naturally going to pull your shoulder down with
it. Let it happen. Your hips and shoulders should be parallel
to your target line, not aimed at it.   When I first started
playing, I hit everything to the right. Much of the time it was
because of a slice or block, but even when I hit it straight, it
went right. I later learned that I had been lining up that way
all along. Remember, your body is to the side of the target
line, so any line drawn from your eyes to the target will be at
a different angle than the one from the ball to the target.
You must make the adjustment.

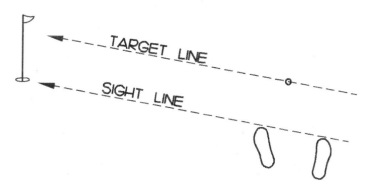

AMATEUR ALIGNMENT

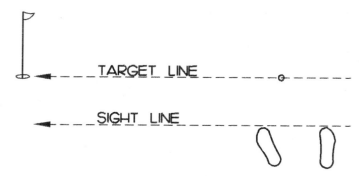

PROPER ALIGNMENT

BALL POSITION

a. *Some golfers say that the 9-iron is hit from a centered stance while each subsequent longer club is played more forward until the driver is played off the left toe.* I never felt comfortable with this because different ball positions produce varying distances from the same club. It is hard to develop a sense for distance as it relates to the club if you have to worry about different ball positions. A consistent ball position will produce consistent shot-making.

b. *Some golfers say that you should swing each club and wherever the club hits the ground is where you set the ball.* I never thought this was a good idea because swinging the club without a ball produces a different spot where the club hits the ground each time. Harvey Penick once said that you should always aim at something when making a practice swing, swinging in the air is great for loosening up, but doesn't help you hitting the ball.

c. *For each club, set the ball 2 to 3 inches inside the instep of your left foot, and adjust the width of your stance with the right foot for each club.* This is good because the ball stays in one position in relation to your left foot. This position will make for consistent shot-making because the club contacts the ball with the shaft at the same angle.

d. *Play every club with the same ball position and width of stance.* This is Greg Norman's stance which is really good for consistent shot-making. He plays the ball off the inside of his left heel and stands with his heels slightly wider than shoulder-width. The only adjustment he has to make is to tilt over a little more as his clubs become shorter.

The key to hitting irons is to contact the ball before the club hits the ground. I personally use a combination of (c) and (d). Irons are generally played 4 to 6 inches inside the left instep while the driver is played 2 to 3 inches inside. With this position, it each club to properly contact the ball; hit down on the ball for short-irons, pick the ball off the grass with mid-irons, and sweep the ball up with the long-irons. The driver is played 2 to 3 inches inside the left heel to guarantee hitting the teed ball on the upswing.

Most beginners release the club too early. If you have trouble properly contacting the ball, try a more centered ball position. By setting the ball more centered in your stance, you will contact the ball with a descending blow. This will help ensure solid contact with the ball. The key point to remember is that the club must strike the ball before it hits the ground. The only time the club hits the ground first, is on sand shots or high lob shots where you are sliding the club under the ball. Try experimenting with various ball positions and use which works best for you.

A big myth that many have ben told is: *moving your ball forward helps reduce your slice.* This is totally opposite of what you should do. A more forward ball position almost guarantees a slice because by the time the club reaches the ball, it will be moving back inside of the target line. This causes an outside-in path which creates a slice. A ball position a few inches inside the front foot will help most beginners hit the ball on the proper swing path.

THE TAKEAWAY

How do you start the swing? This is another one of those subjects for which there is no definitive answer. Some players start with a hip turn or an inward dip with the left knee. Some turn their shoulders while others use the forward press. As we all know by now, a powerful swing is created by good body rotation and lack of tension in the hands, arms and shoulders. The takeaway sets the tone for the entire swing.

I never cared for the forward press because it preset my hands in the wrong position. The deliberate shoulder turn created unwanted tension in my arms and shoulders. Starting the swing with the lower body seems counter-productive to building resistance in the upper body. You have to think of the body as a giant spring that is wound from the top (shoulders and arms). With this in mind, wherever the winding starts, the unwinding ends; if your arms wind first, they should unwind last. This is the proper sequence for a powerful swing.

The club needs to start back with a swing. Swinging doesn't create tension, whereas turning does. Swinging the club back also establishes the proper sequence of the downswing, which is a mirror of the backswing. The proper sequence is: hands—arms—shoulders—hips—hips—shoulders—arms—hands —impact—follow through. Swinging the club back sets up a rhythm and timing for the entire golf swing.

THE BACKSWING

The purpose of the backswing is to reach the *position at the top* while winding up the body. So much has been made about taking the club back on plane that many people concentrate too hard on following that imaginary plane.

Taking the club back on such a deliberate path causes unwanted tension in the arms and shoulders. If you watch some of the tour players, you will see different, sometimes very different, backswings than the so-called traditional teaching. They demonstrate that it is not overly important as to how you reach the position at the top, as long as you get there.

Remember the physics; the bigger the arc of the club, the faster the speed. From the takeaway position, let the club swing up to parallel (like the hands of a clock at nine o'clock) as your shoulders turn to follow the club. At this point, if your arms are relaxed the club shaft should be pointing straight back parallel to the ground with the toe of the club pointing straight up to the sky. Your left arm should be extended (but not rigid) with the back of your firm left wrist facing perpendicular to the target. Your right arm should be relaxed with the elbow hanging down by your side. Notice that your shoulder has already turned to allow for a straight left arm and your weight is naturally shifting to your right side. It is important not to let the weight roll to the outside of your right foot, keep it on your instep. If you swing the club up and your arms are relaxed, this position is automatic. The key thoughts here are to create a wide swing arc, and keep the lower body still.

At this point, allow your wrists to turn up but do not break the rhythm of your backswing. Your thumbs, along with the shaft of the club, should be pointing up. The back of your left wrist should be facing away from your body with your wrists fully cocked. This position will form an "L" between your arms and the club shaft. This early setting of the wrists ensures that the swing incorporates the leverage developed by the uncocking of the wrists during the downswing. Continue turning your shoulders in the same rhythm that your takeaway created until you reach the position at the top. As you turn, try to keep your feet flat on the ground. Power is developed from the resistance of your hips to your shoulders. Try to imagine that your body is a spring being wound up by some giant being pulling and turning your club while your feet are in cement.

WINDING UP THE SPRING

POSITION AT THE TOP

Your body is coiled up and ready to swing. You have built up a tremendous amount of energy from your lower body up, which will be released through the clubhead into the golf ball. Your feet are flat on the ground with most of the weight transferred to your right side. Your shoulders are twisted as far to the right as possible which will create resistance in your hips. This is why it is so important to keep your left foot flat; you're trying to develop resistance between your lower and upper body (winding up the spring). If you are flexible enough, your back will be facing the target with the shaft of the club pointing forward. Since your head is attached to your shoulders, your head will have shifted back as your left shoulder is behind the ball. Try not to let your hands get behind your head. The shaft of the club should be pointing toward the target with the toe pointing down. If you can see the clubhead out of the corner of your eye, chances are you have overswung. This position makes it hard to get the club back on plane thus promoting an outside-in swing path causing a slice. If you watch John Daly, his backswing is unbelievable, but he has the talent to control the club and get it back on plane.

It's important not to keep your arm stiff which adds tension, just keep it firm. If your left arm bends too much, the club will drop behind your head. This promotes an outside-in swing path creating a slice, so keep your hands high. A good way to check the position of the club at the top is to relax your hands and let the club drop:

a.   If it drops on your head, you will make an outside-in slicing swing.

b.   If it drops behind you, your swing will be too flat.

c.   *Ideally it should drop on your shoulder.* When the club is positioned properly, it is easy to let the club drop into the inside-out swing plane that will produce a straight shot.

It is critical to remember that the position at the top is not a point at which to stop the swing, but hold only a fraction of a second pause. You have a decelerating backswing turning into an accelerating downswing. Speed is gradually built as the body uncoils. The best visual aid on this transition was cited by C. Jonathan Shoemaker in a book called "Juggling Golf." Jonathan said when he pushed his daughter on a swing, proper timing was required to gain maximum height. If he pushed too soon, the momentum of the swing would knock him off balance with the mistimed push disrupting the rhythm of the swing. If he pushed too late, he was chasing the swing nearly falling flat on his face. To get that perfect push, he let his fingers lightly catch the swing on the way up. As the swing peaked, he applied gradual building pressure until the swing left his fingers. In this way, he produced the strongest push. If you can visualize this swing, it will help you develop a smooth and rhythmical swing that is important to developing power and consistency.

The transition from backswing to downswing is where many beginners get into trouble. They rush the transition by jerking the club from the top in an effort to swing with power. All this does is to *cast* the club at the ball, which usually brings the club over the top producing a big slice. Also, starting the downswing with the arms also makes the club come over the top. Remember, we don't need the speed at the top, we need it at impact. Watch pros like Ernie Els. He has a fluid like swing that appears almost in slow motion. In reality, he is one of the longest hitters on the tour because he generates a clubhead speed of more than 125 mph. He accomplishes this by building his speed through swinging the club with his arms, not *casting* the clubs violently with his hands.

THE DOWNSWING

Do not start the downswing with your hands! Remember when we talked about throwing a baseball back in the Introduction? The same principle applies to the downswing, we start the downswing from the ground up. To build speed, energy is released gradually from the legs and hips to the shoulders and arms. As your left knee and hips start to rotate to the left, you will naturally start bringing your shoulders around. Your weight will begin to transfer from your right side to your left; this is where your power is developed. When the body uncoils first from the hips, then the shoulders, the centrifugal force of the body unwinding will pull the arms and hands around with it. This is where you let the club drop down naturally and swing through to the finish position. If you let your body do what it wants to do without forcing your arms and hands, you will swing on an inside-out path which will hit the ball straight. To demonstrate, stand with your feet about shoulder width apart. With relaxed arms, twist your hips back and forth. Your arms and shoulders should lag behind your hips as your arms whip back and forth. This is essentially what your downswing is doing. *Let the lower body lead the upper.*

Rick Smith, the well-known teaching pro has said in several articles that to hit the ball straight, no matter what happened to the club during the swing, it had to hit Point A during the downswing. Hitting Point A guaranteed that the swing was locked on the proper plane, thus guaranteeing a good shot. If you miss Point A, it's too late to get the club back on plane. So what is this Point A? Point A is when the club is parallel to the target line and the ground with the butt of the club pointing to the target. This means that the club is lined up with the target and is coming in on plane.

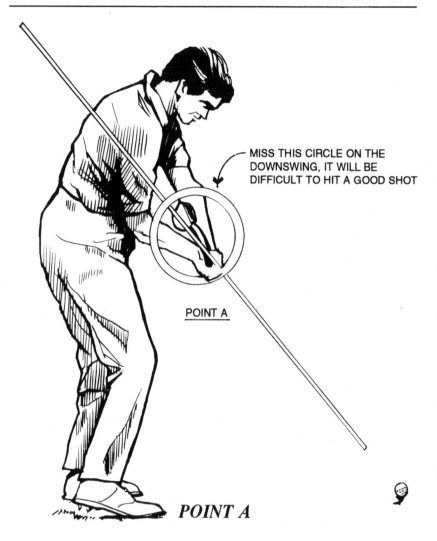

MISS THIS CIRCLE ON THE
DOWNSWING, IT WILL BE
DIFFICULT TO HIT A GOOD SHOT

POINT A

POINT A

An important thought to take with you is: When you start your downswing, try to slowly accelerate the club through impact. It is not necessary to jerk the club down with brute strength; you don't need the speed at the top. Remember, you are building speed with your body, the uncoiling of your hips and shoulders will whip the clubhead through impact. Visualize the little girl on the swing; her maximum speed is at the bottom, not at the top.

IMPACT POSITION

At impact, your legs drive forward as your hip continues to rotate to the left. If you let your body work, your hips will rotate counter-clockwise toward the target with your shoulders slightly behind following your hips. Both arms at impact should be extended with the back of your left hand facing the target. Also, try to keep your left foot flat on the ground. Your right foot will naturally roll up on the ball, so don't fight it. Many times golfers raise up on their toes; this usually means they are trying to help the ball get up in the air with their arms and are probably slowing the club. Being on your toes can lead to sliding which leads to thin shots. If you are on your toes, the solid foundation you created at the set-up is lost. Make that pivot point absolutely centered. Remember, in *Golf Physics, keep a quiet lower body?*

Important point: Don't hit the ball, swing through it!

THE FINISH POSITION

A good finish position is characterized by good balance; most of your weight should be on your left foot with the right foot on its toes. The hips should be square to the target with the left shoulder, hip, knee and top of the foot forming a straight vertical line. The left leg should be straight; if it is bent, you may have slid. The club shaft should be behind your head pointing across your neck to the right with your right shoulder under the chin. It is important to keep your head up and watch the flight of your ball.

If you have done everything right, the momentum of the club after impact will carry you naturally to a finish position. The finish position can tell you much about how you hit the shot; did you finish on balance, are you facing the target, did you allow your weight to transfer? If you missed one of these points, chances are you hit a bad shot. An incomplete finish may lead to an errant or blocked shot that goes to the right because you decelerated your swing.

There are more theories on the full-swing than any other area of golf. It is important for you to learn the basic positions and adapt them to your own swing. An effective golf swing does not have to be a textbook swing. With basic fundamentals you will develop your own style. I had the good fortune to train in the martial arts so I possess great flexibility. But the key points that really helped me develop my own swing were to; *swing the club back* and *start the downswing with my body.* Those two thoughts allowed my body to create the rest of my swing. Some of the best players on the tour have developed their own styles. Lee Trevino takes the club up way outside, loops it at the top and drops it inside. Fred Couples picks up the club with his arms, makes a late shoulder turn, and drops the club inside. Raymond Floyd takes the club way inside, brings it straight up at the shoulder turn, then drops the club inside. These are all great players with different swings, but they have three things in common:

1. *They hit the position at the top.*

2. *They hit Point A on the downswing.*

3. *They hit great shots!*

KEY POINTS

Setup Position

1. Feet shoulder width apart, weight 50/50 on balls of feet

2. Turn out left foot 15 to 20 degrees

3. Bend from hips 20 to 30 degrees and keep head up

4. Arms hang straight down to neutral grip

Takeaway

1. Swing club back

2. Maintain quiet lower body

3. Create wide swing arc

Backswing

1. Rotate shoulder as much as possible

2. Keep feet flat on the ground

3. Keep left arm firm but not tense

4. Allow weight to transfer to right foot

Position at the Top

1. Weight transfers to right foot

2. Hold hands up high over right shoulder

Downswing

1. Start with lower body and turn left hip out

2. Allow right arm to drop down

3. Allow arms and shoulders to follow hips

4. Hit Position A

5. Allow weight to transfer to the left foot

Finish Position

1. Hips are square to the target

2. 90 percent of your weight is transferred to the left foot

3. Arms finish across your body

KEY THOUGHT

Swing through the ball; don't hit it!

Full Swing: Setup Position

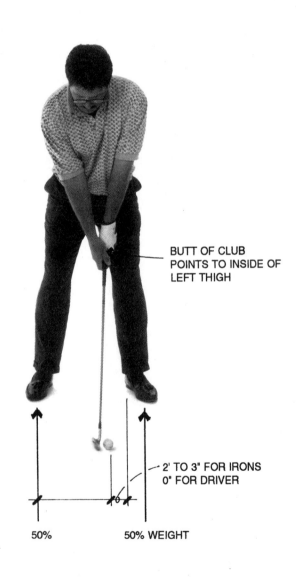

BUTT OF CLUB
POINTS TO INSIDE OF
LEFT THIGH

2' TO 3" FOR IRONS
0" FOR DRIVER

50%   50% WEIGHT

Full Swing: Setup Position

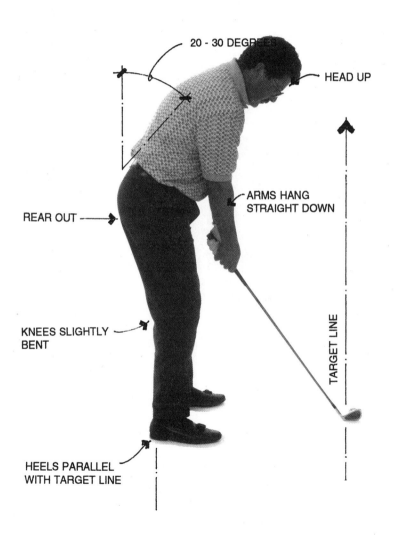

20 - 30 DEGREES

HEAD UP

ARMS HANG
STRAIGHT DOWN

REAR OUT

KNEES SLIGHTLY
BENT

TARGET LINE

HEELS PARALLEL
WITH TARGET LINE

Full Swing: Takeaway Position

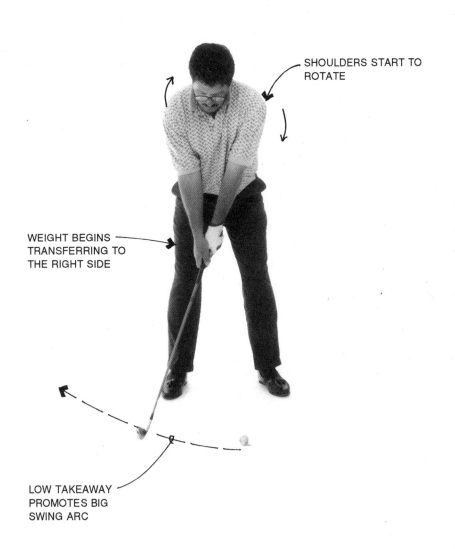

SHOULDERS START TO
ROTATE

WEIGHT BEGINS
TRANSFERRING TO
THE RIGHT SIDE

LOW TAKEAWAY
PROMOTES BIG
SWING ARC

Full Swing: Takeaway Position

HEAD UP

SWING PLANE

CLUB STAYS
UNDERNEATH
SWING PLANE

Full Swing: Halfway Position

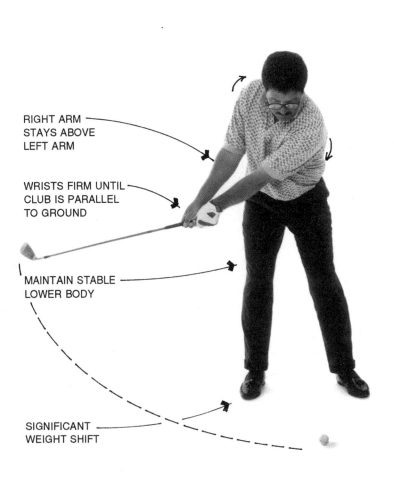

RIGHT ARM
STAYS ABOVE
LEFT ARM

WRISTS FIRM UNTIL
CLUB IS PARALLEL
TO GROUND

MAINTAIN STABLE
LOWER BODY

SIGNIFICANT
WEIGHT SHIFT

Full Swing: Halfway Position

DON'T DIP YOUR HEAD, KEEP IT UP

MAINTAIN TRIANGLE

WRISTS CAN NOW UNHINGE

Full Swing: Position at the Top

WRISTS COCKED

WEIGHT FULLY
TRANSFERRED

70%   30% WEIGHT

Full Swing: Position at the Top

HANDS OVER RIGHT SHOULDER

SHOULDERS FULLY
TURNED 90°

RESIST WITH HIPS—ALLOW HIPS TO
SLIGHTLY TURN

BODY IS COMPLETELY COILED—READY TO GO!

Full Swing: Downswing

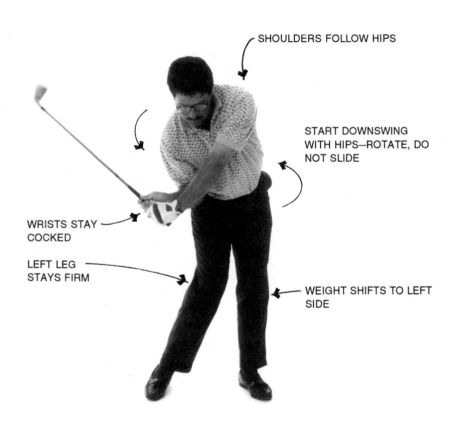

SHOULDERS FOLLOW HIPS

START DOWNSWING
WITH HIPS—ROTATE, DO
NOT SLIDE

WRISTS STAY
COCKED

LEFT LEG
STAYS FIRM

WEIGHT SHIFTS TO LEFT
SIDE

Full Swing: Downswing Hitting Point A

LEFT ARM FIRM

CLUB IS COMING IN
UNDER PLANE

Full Swing: Impact Position

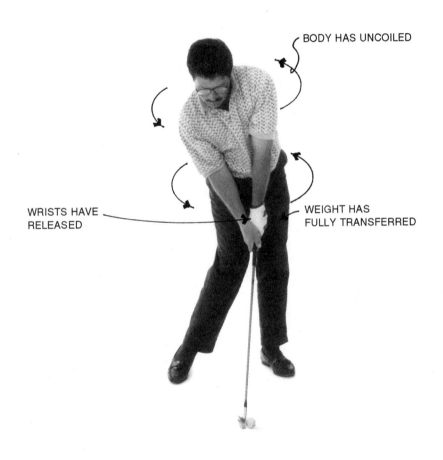

BODY HAS UNCOILED

WRISTS HAVE
RELEASED

WEIGHT HAS
FULLY TRANSFERRED

Full Swing: Follow-Through

TRIANGLE MAINTAINED

ARMS EXTENDED

Full Swing: Finish Position

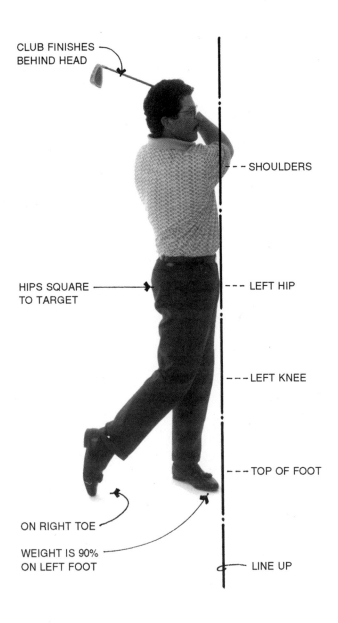

CLUB FINISHES
BEHIND HEAD

- - - SHOULDERS

HIPS SQUARE
TO TARGET

- - - LEFT HIP

- - - LEFT KNEE

- - - TOP OF FOOT

ON RIGHT TOE

WEIGHT IS 90%
ON LEFT FOOT

LINE UP

Full Swing: Finish Position

WATCHING BALL
LAND ON GREEN

HIPS SQUARE
TO TARGET

WEIGHT FULLY TRANSFERRED

Full Swing: Finish Position

CLUB BEHIND HEAD

FINISH ON RIGHT TOE

CHAPTER SIX

THE SHORT GAME
The Key to Scoring

Playing a round of golf, over sixty per cent of all your shots will be a pitch, chip or putt. As a typical weekend golfer, this is probably the weakest part of your game. Yet it is the part that most golfers rarely practice. When visiting a driving range, you see ninety percent of the people practicing the full swing, *driving the ball.* Maybe this is where the name *driving range* came from. You rarely see anyone spending much time practicing their chips and putts. Any pro will tell you, improvement in this area is the key to lowering your scores.

A recent trip to Pebble Beach for the AT&T Championship was the first time I watched the pros compete live. The whole atmosphere and scenery of the event were enough to make anyone a golf enthusiast. What impressed me the most while watching the pros wasn't that they were long off the tee; what was most impressive was their short game. Their control and accuracy was amazing in their approach shots to the greens. This is where the tour players separate themselves from the amateurs. On shots inside of 50 yards, most tour players can put the ball within six feet of the pin on a regular basis while most amateurs are happy just to get on the green. The pro player's ability to shape shots: hit a control fade or draw and hit high or low shots are concepts most amateurs can't even think about.

In reviewing statistics on how players score during a round, it is clear that an improvement in the short game is the key to lowering scores. When comparing a scratch golfer (zero handicap) to a bogey golfer (18 handicap), the scratch golfer:

a. Will average 17 more yards off the tee and hit two more fairways than the bogey golfer.

b. On approach shots will hit twelve out of eighteen greens in regulation while a bogey will hit only four.

c. Is three times more likely to put the ball within five feet of the hole inside of 50 yards than a bogey. To make matters worse, bogey golfers are five times more likely to completely miss the greens.

d. Is four times more likely to recover from a bunker than a bogey.

e. Will average six one-putts while the bogey will average two.

The moral of the story, *practice your approach shots and short game to lower your score.* The short game can be broken down into four sections

1. *Pitching:* In its simplified form, this applies to anything other than a full swing. Most of these shots are inside of 75 yards.

2. *Sand Shot:* Shot out of a bunker around a green. For the short game sequence, we will only concentrate on greenside bunkers.

3. *Chipping or Chip Shot:* Shot used for a ball just off the green where using a putter is not practical.

4. *Putting:* Used for any ball on the green.

THE PITCH SHOT

The pitch shot is an accurate scoring shot that is key to lowering your scores. If you are a bogey golfer, chances are you are going to miss a lot of greens. Most bogey golfers only hit an average of four greens in regulation. When you miss a green, the pitch shot is doubly important in trying to salvage par.

A good pitch starts with a good wedge. As discussed previously, your wedge has to feel comfortable during your swing and provide plenty of feedback to develop a *feel* for distance and trajectory. I prefer a sand wedge because of its heavy sole which allows me a certain margin for error, but a pitching wedge or loft wedge will most certainly work.

THE SETUP POSITION

Like any shot in golf, it begins with a good setup position. Your feet are squared with your weight 50/50 on the balls of your feet. Your stance is around four inches less than shoulder width apart. The ball is placed dead center in your stance with your hands hanging straight down and relaxed. The shaft of your club is pointing at your belt buckle. The important point here is that your **arms remain very relaxed and your hands stay soft**. If everything is correct, the ball, your hands, sternum and head should all line up centered in your stance. The key point to remember for the pitch shot setup is **center, center, center**.

THE BACKSWING

Like the full swing, the takeaway should begin with a slight swing of the club. This ensures that no tension develops from a too deliberate takeaway. Continue to take the club back with your shoulders while keeping a very still lower body. You are trying to buildup resistance between your upper and lower body. There should also be very little weight shift to the back foot. As the club shaft approaches parallel or point A, begin to cock your wrists early so that by the time the shaft is parallel to the ground, the club shaft is pointing straight up. This is the L position that is so important to pitching. A good way to check your position is make sure your thumbs are pointing straight up, and the back of your left hand is facing straight away from your body. Your hands at the top of the backswing should never be below your waist or above your shoulders. It's important to remember that your wrists work up and down, not side to side. To get this feeling, from the setup position, lift the club up and down with just your wrists while leaving the hands where they are.

It is important to strike the ball while the clubhead is accelerating, never decelerate the club into the ball. Many times golfers make a last second decision during the swing. If they feel that they're swinging too hard, then they try to decelerate the club almost always resulting in a sculled shot.

THE DOWNSWING

Like the full swing, the downswing is initiated with the hips. Even though the lower body is very still, the swing is initiated by rotating or turning the hips as you let your weight start shifting forward. Let your arms drop to let the clubhead drop to the ground. The idea is to bounce the club off the ground (a sand wedge works well for this shot). If your setup was correct, the club should bottom out at the center of your stance sliding under the golf ball pitching it high and soft. *It is important to have soft hands;* this will allow your hands to turn over properly and it will allow the club to do what it was designed to do. Fat shots or sculled shots are usually the result of trying to guide the club too much with your hands.

THE FINISH POSITION

The finish position is similar to the full-swing position in that most of your weight will have transferred to your front foot, and your hips and shoulders will be square to the target. Instead of finishing with your hands up over your left shoulder as you did in the full swing, simply let your right arm cross your chest, and let the club settle to your left side. The club shaft should be pointing straight up in the air, your right forearm parallel to the ground, and the back of your right hand facing the target. It should be a mirror image of your position at the backswing. You are swinging from L-position to L-position. As you hit the shot, allow your eyes to follow the ball. This helps in developing a feel for distance. Remember, this is a very relaxed rhythmical shot that is developed by feel and tempo. Varying distances will be achieved by the length of the backswing, and the tempo of the swing.

A slow tempo is used for a short shot while a faster one is used for shots requiring more distance. The speed of your hip turn controls the distance for this shot. Rhythm and tempo are constantly mentioned because these are the components that control the speed of the turn. Before the pros play this shot, those mini-swings they are making help them adjust their rhythm and tempo for the shot.

There are a multitude of pitch shot variations that the low-handicap players will use to _work the course._ That means imparting draws, fades, and high or low spin on the ball. A skilled player can shape the ball toward the greens to ensure the best angle of approach. He or she can also impart controlled spinning of the ball to work the greens. Most all of these shots require great skill and practice.

It is recommended that the beginning player stay with the basic variations to the standard pitch shot; the pitch and run, and the high lob shot. As you gain confidence and develop a feel for the standard pitches, then you can begin the fine tuning of your shotmaking by learning to shape your shots.

In this chapter, we will stay with the basic variations.

PITCH SHOT KEY POINTS

Setup Position

1. Feet less than shoulder width apart, weight 50/50 on balls of feet

2. Ball, shaft, hands and sternum are centered

Swing

1. Rotate shoulders and cock wrists early

2. Little weight shift on backswing to L position

3. Initiate swing with hips and bounce the club off the ground

4. Keep arms relaxed, hands soft, and allow the club to finish on the left side

5. Shift weight forward with hips and shoulders that square to the target to finish in balance

6. Allow your eyes to follow the ball

KEY THOUGHT

Keep hands soft and make rhythmical swing

Pitch Shot: Setup Position

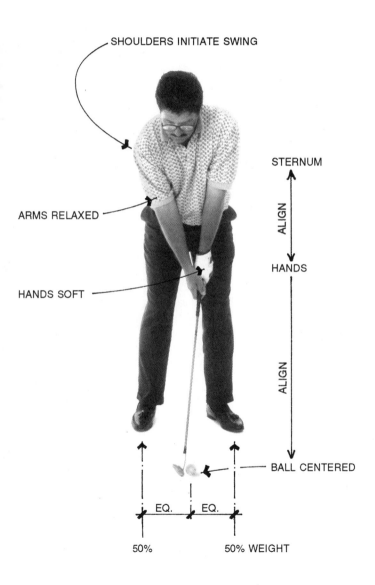

SHOULDERS INITIATE SWING

ARMS RELAXED

HANDS SOFT

STERNUM

ALIGN

HANDS

ALIGN

BALL CENTERED

EQ.   EQ.

50%   50% WEIGHT

Pitch Shot: Backswing Position

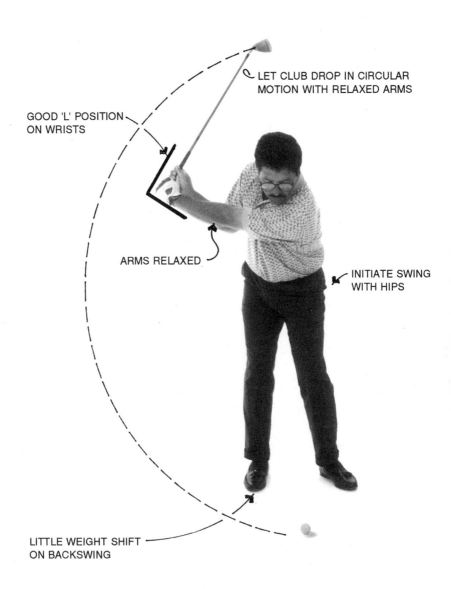

LET CLUB DROP IN CIRCULAR MOTION WITH RELAXED ARMS

GOOD 'L' POSITION ON WRISTS

ARMS RELAXED

INITIATE SWING WITH HIPS

LITTLE WEIGHT SHIFT ON BACKSWING

Pitch Shot: Impact Position

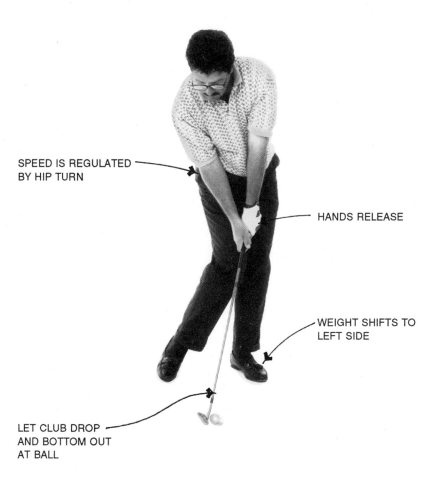

SPEED IS REGULATED
BY HIP TURN

HANDS RELEASE

WEIGHT SHIFTS TO
LEFT SIDE

LET CLUB DROP
AND BOTTOM OUT
AT BALL

Pitch Shot: Finish Position

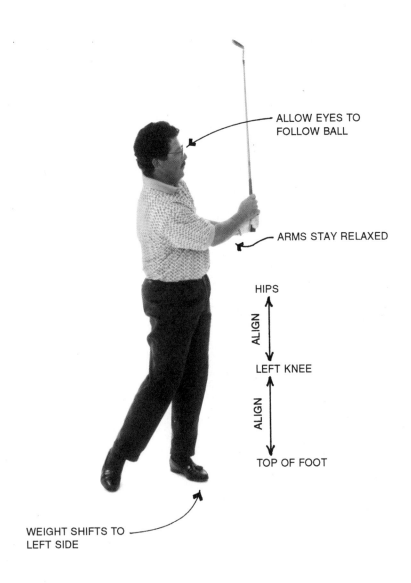

ALLOW EYES TO
FOLLOW BALL

ARMS STAY RELAXED

HIPS

ALIGN

LEFT KNEE

ALIGN

TOP OF FOOT

WEIGHT SHIFTS TO
LEFT SIDE

Pitch Shot: Finish Position

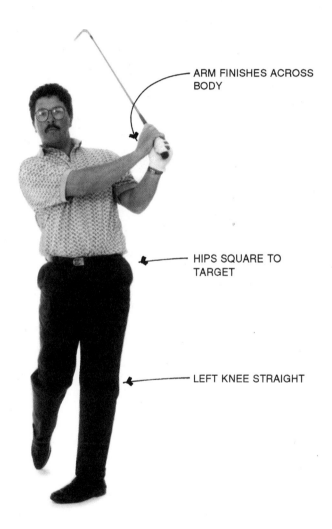

ARM FINISHES ACROSS BODY

HIPS SQUARE TO TARGET

LEFT KNEE STRAIGHT

PITCH SHOT VARIATIONS

PITCH AND RUN

The pitch and run is a low-flying shot that will stay low and roll a greater distance after it hits the ground than a normal pitch. This is used when you have a lot of green to work with enabling you to roll the ball up to the pin. Most golfers have learned to use this shot after hitting from under a tree branch after a badly sliced tee shot. To hit this shot, minor variations to the standard pitch are required.

THE SETUP POSITION

Take your normal pitching stance with more of your weight on your left side. The ball is placed back in your stance, lining up off your right instep. The shaft of your club points at your left hip, with your center ahead of the ball. *The shaft will always point toward the leg that is more weighted.*

THE BACKSWING

The takeaway should begin as a standard pitch. Continue to take the club back with your shoulders while keeping a very still lower body. Your weight remains on your left leg. The big difference with this shot is that there will be no cocking of the wrists. When the club shaft reaches parallel or Point A, do not cock the wrists up. A good way to check your position is to make sure your left arm and the club shaft are pointing straight back, and the back of your left hand is facing straight away from your body.

THE DOWNSWING

Like the standard pitch, the downswing is initiated with the hips. The lower body remains very still as your weight stays forward. If your set up was correct, the club will strike the ball with a descending blow. Continue to let your weight fully transfer to your left side as your hips and shoulders square to the target.

THE FINISH POSITION

After striking the ball, allow your right hand to turn over with both hands finishing waist high. If everything went okay, your hips and shoulders should be square to the target, your weight will be fully transferred to your left side, and the shaft of the club will be pointing at the target. A good way to ensure that your hands properly turn over is to finish with the toe of the club pointing to the left, and the back of your right hand facing the sky.

PITCH AND RUN

Used for hitting under tree limbs or when you have plenty of green to work with. Skilled players often play a bump and run, where they bump the ball into the side of a hill slowing the ball allowing it to roll easily onto the green.

PITCH AND RUN KEY POINTS

Setup Position

1. Ball is positioned back in the stance

2. 60 to 70 percent of your weight is on your left leg

3. Hands are opposite left thigh with shaft pointing to the left hip

4. Your center is ahead of the ball

Swing

1. Similar to standard pitch

2. Little or no wrist cock

3. Let club finish waist high pointing toward the target

4. Finish with toe of club pointing left and the back of your right hand facing the sky

KEY THOUGHT

Strike ball with a descending blow

Pitch and Run: Setup Position

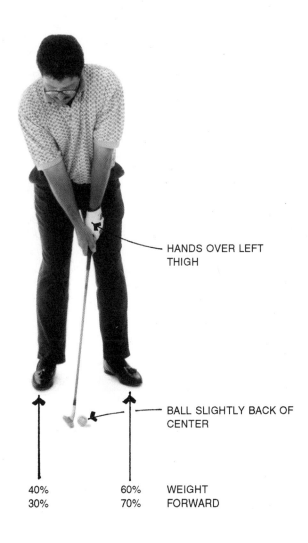

HANDS OVER LEFT THIGH

BALL SLIGHTLY BACK OF CENTER

| 40% | 60% | WEIGHT |
| 30% | 70% | FORWARD |

Pitch and Run: Backswing

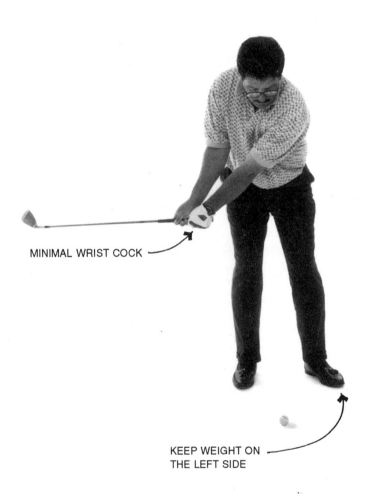

MINIMAL WRIST COCK

KEEP WEIGHT ON
THE LEFT SIDE

Pitch and Run: Impact Position

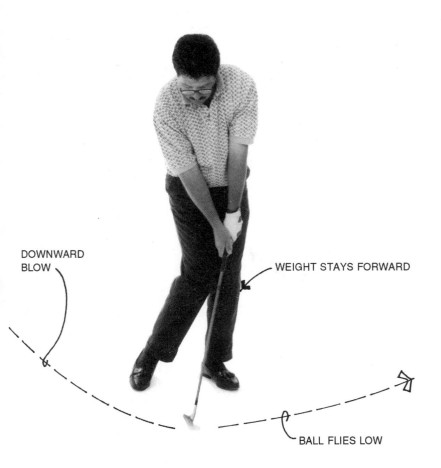

DOWNWARD
BLOW

WEIGHT STAYS FORWARD

BALL FLIES LOW

Pitch and Run: Finish Position

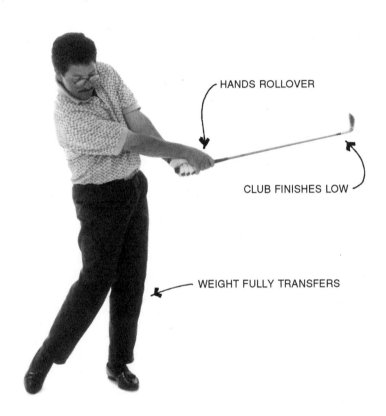

HANDS ROLLOVER

CLUB FINISHES LOW

WEIGHT FULLY TRANSFERS

Pitch and Run: Finish Position

HEAD DOWN
UNTIL AFTER
SHOT

HANDS ROLLOVER

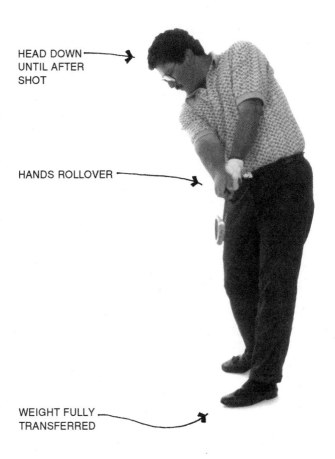

WEIGHT FULLY
TRANSFERRED

PITCH SHOT VARIATIONS

THE HIGH LOB SHOT

The lob shot is a high shot that lands softly with little roll. This shot is used if you have to hit over a bunker or hazard with very little green to work with. This shot lifts the ball high and drops it softly onto the green with minimal roll.

THE SETUP POSITION

Your stance should still be around four inches less than shoulder width apart, but should be open about 15 degrees to the left with more of your weight on your right side. The ball is placed forward in your stance, lining up inside your left instep. The shaft of your club points back at your belt buckle, the clubface squared to the target. Your center is behind the ball. *The shaft will always point toward the weighted side.*

THE BACKSWING

The takeaway begins as a standard pitch. Continue to take the club back with your shoulders while keeping a very still lower body. Your weight remains toward your right leg. As the club shaft reaches parallel or Point A, begin to cock your wrists early so that by the time the shaft is parallel to the ground, the club shaft is pointing straight up.

THE DOWNSWING

Like the standard pitch, the downswing is initiated with the hips. Even though the lower body is very still, the swing is initiated by rotating or turning the hips as you let your weight start shifting forward. Let your arms drop down to let the clubhead bounce off the ground behind the ball. If your setup was correct, the club should bottom out behind the ball and slide under the golf ball pitching it high and soft. Continue to let your weight fully transfer to your left side as your hips and shoulders square to the target. *It is important to have soft hands and relaxed arms to let the club slide under the ball.*

THE FINISH POSITION

The finish position is similar to the standard pitch in that most of your weight is transferred to your front foot, and your hips and shoulders are square to the target. The club finishes on your left side with your right arm across your chest. This shot finishes like a standard pitch.

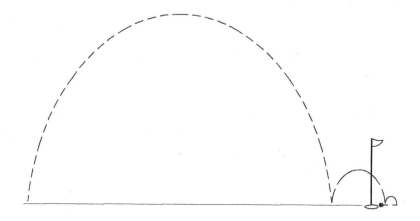

HIGH LOB SHOT

HIGH LOB SHOT KEY POINTS

Setup Position

1. Ball is positioned forward in an open stance

2. 60 to 70 percent of your weight is on your right leg

3. Hands and your center are positioned slightly behind the ball

4. The butt of your club is pointing at your belt buckle

Swing

1. Rotate shoulders and cock wrists early

2. Weight stays back on backswing to L position

3. Initiate swing with hips and slide clubhead under ball

4. Keep arms relaxed, hands soft, and allow club to finish on the left side

5. Weight shifts forward with hips and shoulders that square to the target to finish in balance

6. Allow your eyes to follow the ball

KEY THOUGHT

Bounce club off ground and slide under ball

High Lob Shot: Setup Position

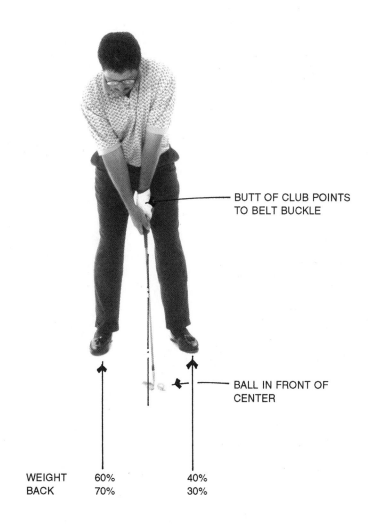

BUTT OF CLUB POINTS
TO BELT BUCKLE

BALL IN FRONT OF
CENTER

WEIGHT   60%   40%
BACK   70%   30%

High Lob Shot: Backswing

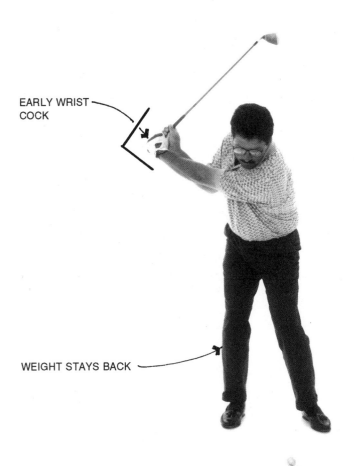

EARLY WRIST
COCK

WEIGHT STAYS BACK

High Lob Shot: Impact Position

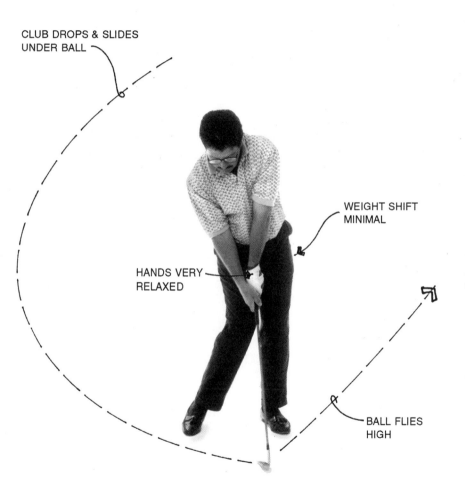

CLUB DROPS & SLIDES
UNDER BALL

WEIGHT SHIFT
MINIMAL

HANDS VERY
RELAXED

BALL FLIES
HIGH

High Lob Shot: Finish Position

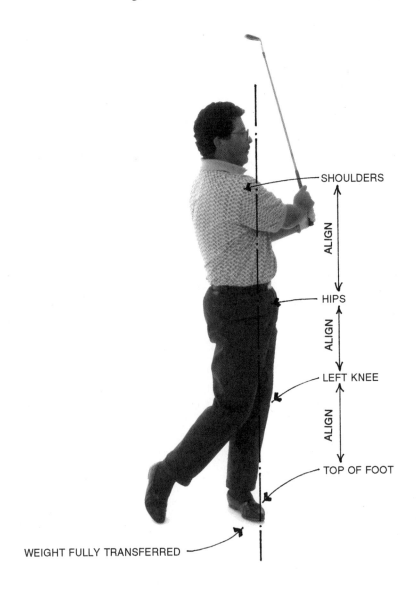

SHOULDERS

ALIGN

HIPS

ALIGN

LEFT KNEE

ALIGN

TOP OF FOOT

WEIGHT FULLY TRANSFERRED

THE SAND SHOT

The greenside bunker shot is probably the most misunderstood shot that a high handicapper faces. Most golfers make this shot much harder than it really is. I remember the times I hit into a greenside bunker; it was that "*Oh _hit!*" reaction. My friends told me to swing hard and hit behind the ball. I would then make a very hard swing, generally with my arms aiming for a spot a couple of inches behind the ball. By swinging too hard and using my hands, one of three things happened:

1. I hit right behind the ball with no sand getting the ball out, but sending it well over the green.

2. I hit too far behind the ball burying the clubhead and moving a large pile of sand that pushed the ball into the lip of the bunker. This compounded the problem.

3. I hit just where I was aiming, but due to my too hard swing the clubhead would dig into the sand and lift the ball out along with a bucket of sand. Everyone around me said, "*At least you got it out!*"

Once I learned the proper way to hit this shot, it became very easy. I no longer feared the greenside bunkers. Many pros intentionally hit into some bunkers. It is often easier to get up and down out of a bunker, than the deep rough that surrounds the greens. The sand shot is nothing more than a high lob pitch shot with slight variations in the setup. Once you get over the mental hurdle of this shot, you will find it fairly easy.

SETUP POSITION

The setup for the sand shot is similar to the high lob shot, the only difference being a 50/50 weight distribution. The first thing to do is open up your club face. Rotate the face of the club to approximately the one o'clock position and regrip the club. It is important to regrip the club after you've rotated it and not twist your wrists; your grip will tend to square at impact. Stand about shoulder width apart with your weight 50/50 and play the ball off your left instep. You will notice that your open clubface is pointing to the right of your target. To compensate for this, simply aim your body to the left until your clubface is squared to the target. If your setup is correct, your body should be aligned to the eleven o'clock position, and your hands, sternum and center will be behind the ball. The last thing to remember is to dig your feet in; you want to be sure to set your feet and level yourself.

THE BACKSWING

The takeaway begins as a standard pitch. Continue to take the club back with your shoulders while keeping a very still lower body. There should be virtually no weight shift during the backswing. Your wrists should be fully cocked by the time the shaft is parallel to the ground.

THE DOWNSWING

Like the standard pitch, the downswing is initiated with the hips. Even though the lower body is very still, the swing is initiated by rotating or turning the hips as your weight starts shifting forward. With a slightly firmer grip, allow the club to bounce off the sand. You are trying to bounce the flange of the club two to three inches behind the ball. If your setup was correct, the club should bottom out at the center of your stance lifting a handful of sand and the ball out of the bunker. *It is important to allow your body to pull you around and not allow your hands to take over.*

THE FINISH POSITION

The finish position is similar to the standard pitch in that most of your weight is transferred to your front foot, and your hips and shoulders are square to the target. The club finishes on your left side with your right arm across your chest. This shot finishes like a standard pitch. It is very important on the sand shot to complete the downswing, and hold your position until the ball stops.

The secret to the greenside bunker shot is to make a full-pitch swing. Shortening or decelerating the swing is a sure way to hit a thin shot. Make an aggressive swing, but not a stronger swing. Keep a firmer grip and maintain your tempo.

SAND SHOT KEY POINTS

Setup Position

1. Feet dug into sand with an open stance, shoulder width apart with weight 50/50

2. Ball is positioned off left heel, hands and sternum are behind ball

3. Clubface open

Swing

1. Rotate shoulders and cock wrists early

2. No weight shift on backswing to L position

3. Initiate swing with hips, bounce flange of club off the sand 2 to 3 inches behind the ball

4. Make complete swing with a firmer grip

5. Weight shifts forward with hips and shoulders square to target

6. Finish in balance with club on left side

KEY THOUGHT

Bounce the club off the sand with a complete swing

Sand Shot: Setup Position

WEIGHT 50/50

DIG FEET DOWN INTO
THE SAND UNTIL
FIRMLY SET

BALL INSIDE OF LEFT
HEEL (GOOD LIE ONLY)

Sand Shot: Setup Position

TARGET LINE

CLUBFACE—SQUARE TO TARGET

FEET ALIGNED 15° TO 20° LEFT

Sand Shot: Backswing Position

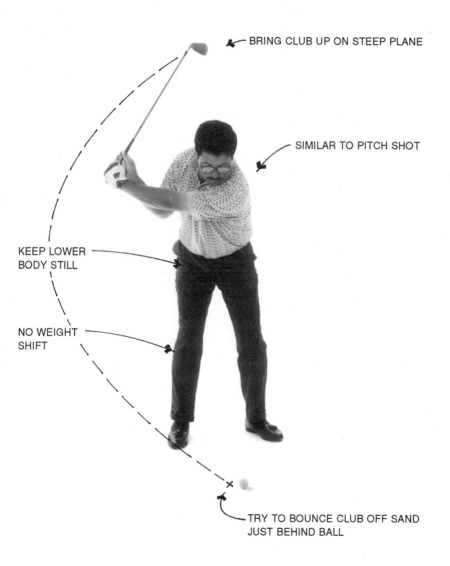

BRING CLUB UP ON STEEP PLANE

SIMILAR TO PITCH SHOT

KEEP LOWER
BODY STILL

NO WEIGHT
SHIFT

TRY TO BOUNCE CLUB OFF SAND
JUST BEHIND BALL

Sand Shot: Impact Position

MAKE AGGRESSIVE SWING!

INITIATE SWING
WITH HIPS

HANDS STAY
FIRMER

BOUNCE CLUB OFF
SAND BEHIND BALL

Sand Shot: Finish Position

WEIGHT FULLY
TRANSFERRED

FINISHES LIKE PITCH SHOT

SAND SHOT VARIATIONS

THE BURIED LIE SHOT

The other problem encountered with bunker shots is the buried lie. This happens when the ball is stuck down in the sand with only a small portion visible. It is not necessary to swing very hard to get this ball out; you only need to make an adjustment in your setup.

THE SETUP POSITION

Your feet should be shoulder width apart with more of your weight on your left side. The club is squared up with your stance. The ball is placed back in your stance, slightly back of center. The shaft of your club is pointing at the inside of your left thigh, with your center ahead of the ball.

THE BACKSWING

The takeaway begins as a standard pitch. Continue to take the club back with your shoulders while keeping a very still lower body. Your weight remains toward your left leg. As the club shaft reaches parallel or Point A, begin to cock your wrists early so that by the time the shaft is parallel to the ground, the club shaft is pointing straight up.

THE DOWNSWING

Like the standard pitch, the downswing is initiated with the hips. With this shot, try to rotate the hips as much as possible on the downswing to ensure the club will not get hung up in the sand. Let your arms drop down with a firm grip to let the leading edge of the clubface strike directly behind the ball, digging it out. Continue to let your weight fully transfer to your left side as your hips and shoulders square to the target. *It is important to hit down behind the ball with a descending blow using the leading edge of the clubface.*

THE FINISH POSITION

The finish position is similar to the pitch and run in that the club finishes low due to the heavy impact of sand. Most of your weight is transferred to your front foot, and your hips and shoulders are square to the target. The club finishes low pointing toward the target with the toe pointing to the left.

BURIED LIE KEY POINTS

Setup Position

1. Ball is positioned back in the stance

2. 60 to 70 percent of your weight is on your left leg

3. Hands and your center are positioned slightly ahead of the ball

4. Clubface is squared to slightly closed

Swing

1. Rotate shoulders and cock wrists early

2. Weight stays forward on backswing to L position

3. Initiate swing with hips, and strike down behind ball with a descending blow

4. Rotate body as much as possible on forward swing

5. Weight shifts forward with hips and shoulders that square to the target to finish in balance

6. Club finishes low

KEY THOUGHT

Rotate your body as much as possible on downswing

Buried Lie Shot: Setup Position

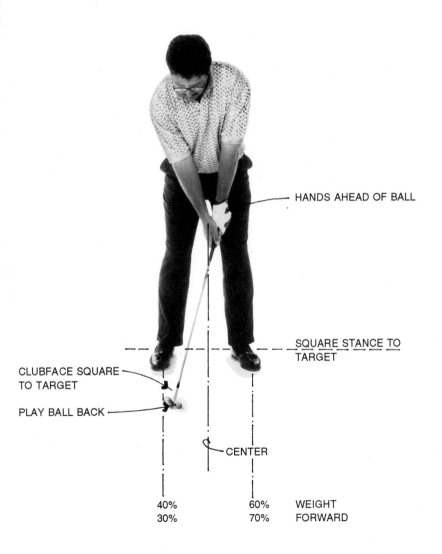

HANDS AHEAD OF BALL

SQUARE STANCE TO TARGET

CLUBFACE SQUARE TO TARGET

PLAY BALL BACK

CENTER

40%   60%   WEIGHT
30%   70%   FORWARD

Buried Lie Shot: Backswing

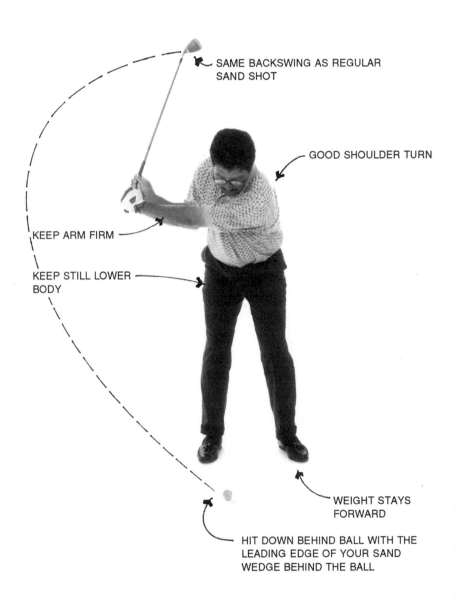

SAME BACKSWING AS REGULAR SAND SHOT

GOOD SHOULDER TURN

KEEP ARM FIRM

KEEP STILL LOWER BODY

WEIGHT STAYS FORWARD

HIT DOWN BEHIND BALL WITH THE LEADING EDGE OF YOUR SAND WEDGE BEHIND THE BALL

Buried Lie Shot: Impact Position

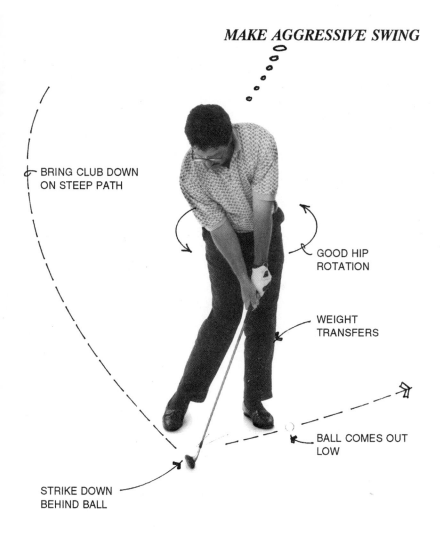

MAKE AGGRESSIVE SWING

BRING CLUB DOWN
ON STEEP PATH

GOOD HIP
ROTATION

WEIGHT
TRANSFERS

BALL COMES OUT
LOW

STRIKE DOWN
BEHIND BALL

Buried Lie Shot: Finish Position

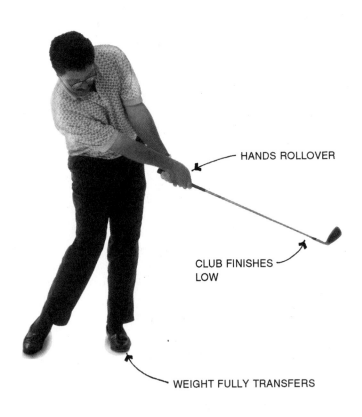

HANDS ROLLOVER

CLUB FINISHES
LOW

WEIGHT FULLY TRANSFERS

THE CHIP SHOT

The chip shot is a low-running shot that is used just off the green. It is designed to carry the ball over uneven ground or rough grass to the green, then roll onto the green to the pin. A good chip shot will produce minimum air time and maximum roll. It's not uncommon to put the ball in the hole since this is an accurate scoring shot. A general rule for all golf shots is: *The longer the ball is up in the air, the more difficult it is to be accurate.* For the high handicap golfer, a general rule of thumb is to putt the ball whenever possible, provided the grass between the ball and green is smooth and even. If it does not allow a putt, then you have to use the chip shot. If you are still too far for a chip, then use a pitch shot.

The chip shot can be taken with almost any club; the perfect chip will fly minimally in the air and stay low, then drop onto the green and roll into the cup. The club you select depends on how far it is to the pin, and how much rough must be cleared before the green. You can use any club from a sand wedge to a 5-wood; I've seen Chi Chi Rodriguez chip with a wood. Obviously, a more lofted club will fly higher and roll less. You have to experiment with the different clubs to get a feel for how far each will carry with your chipping stroke.

The chip shot is not as hard as most beginners think. I see more players having difficulty with this shot by trying to decelerate their swing on this stroke. The easiest way to think of the chip is that; *It is nothing more than a putt with a lofted club.*

THE SETUP POSITION

The key to remember for a chip shot is that the ball must be struck with a descending blow. This is to prevent the *chili-dip;* when the club first bounces on the ground losing pace resulting in a short ball that may not reach the green—or the dreaded *sculled shot;* when the leading edge of the club strikes the ball and sends it rolling off the other side of the green.

The chip and putt differ greatly from the full swing and pitch in that very little body is used. Both chip and putt use a *pendulum swing* that is generated almost entirely from the shoulders, arms and hands. This eliminates the rotation and twisting of the body that could cause a sideways spin on the ball. The ball should roll and spin in the direction it is aimed. The only difference between the putt and chip swings are, in the putt; the wrists stay firm, in the chip; the wrists hinge slightly.

THE STANCE

A proper stance makes it easy to achieve the descending blow required for a chip shot. First, place your feet about twelve inches apart in a slightly open stance. Turn your left toe out slightly, then shift eighty to ninety percent of your weight to the left side, *and keep it there.* Place the ball off your right big toe, two to three clubheads away from the end of your toe. Grip down on the shaft until your left forearm is fairly aligned with the club shaft; your right elbow should be tucked neatly against the right side of your stomach. With your weight forward and the ball back, your hands should be over your left thigh away from your body. Your left arm should be aligned with the shaft of the club. Your head should be over your left toe and your shoulders should be level.

THE PENDULUM STROKE

It's called the pendulum stroke because it works just like a pendulum; the club goes straight back and straight forward with no turning of the club. The shoulders work up and down as they rotate in a *linear motion,* not a circular one. Linear motion is important to keep the path of the backswing and downswing aligned from the ball to the target. The lower body remains very still with no shifting of the weight. The length of the backswing should match the length of the follow-through as distance is controlled by the length of the backswing. Try to keep the follow-through low to the ground pushing both hands forward.

The chipping motion brings the club up quickly on a straight line back. The left shoulder starts dipping as the right starts rising. Keep the left forearm aligned with the shaft and let the right arm fold with the elbow against your side.

As you swing down, reverse the action keeping your weight to the left side. The club comes down on a steeper plane so it picks the ball cleanly off the grass. The clubhead does not accelerate through the shot, it just duplicates the tempo of the backswing. At impact, the back of the left hand and right palm should be facing the target. With a slight chopping motion, the club will strike the ball in a descending blow and will push the ball away before the club skims the ground. Your right elbow skims your stomach as you swing through. On long chips, the left wrist hinges only slightly on the upswing, then unhinges on the downswing.

It is important to follow through with the shot. Let your left shoulder rise as the right shoulder dips, keeping the left arm away from your body with the back of your hand facing toward the target. Continue to let the right arm push the left as both arms are nearly fully extended. This keeps the follow-through low and flat. When the stroke is completed, hold the finish position and follow the ball by turning your head.

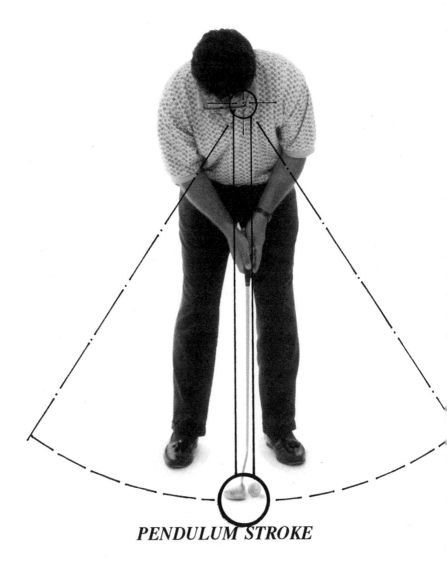

PENDULUM STROKE

It is important to keep the back of the left and the palm of the right hand facing the target line along with the path of the stroke.

CHIP SHOT KEY POINTS

Setup Position

1. Feet about 12 inches apart, slightly open stance

2. 80 to 90 percent of the weight on the left side

3. Ball aligned off the right big toe, two to three clubheads away from the end of the toe

4. Grip down on the shaft with the hands centered over left thigh away from the body.

5. Club shaft aligned with left forearm while right is tucked against right side

6. Head over left foot

Stroke

1. Rotate shoulders with a rocking motion in a linear, not circular plane

2. Strike ball with a descending chopping blow as clubhead stays on target line

3. Wrists hinge slightly on upswing, then unhinge on downswing keeping the left forearm aligned with club shaft

4. Allow right hand to control stroke with left elbow brushing stomach on stroke

5. Keep a still lower body with weight on left side throughout stroke

6. Clubhead finishes low as position is held

7. Follow ball by turning head, not the body

KEY THOUGHT

No weight shift, keep weight to left side throughout stroke

Chip Shot: Setup Position

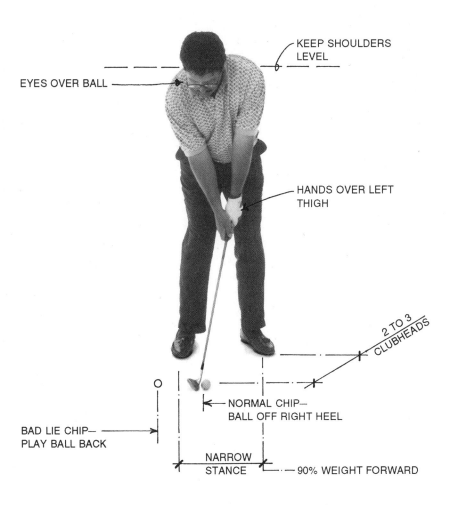

KEEP SHOULDERS LEVEL

EYES OVER BALL

HANDS OVER LEFT THIGH

2 TO 3 CLUBHEADS

NORMAL CHIP— BALL OFF RIGHT HEEL

BAD LIE CHIP— PLAY BALL BACK

NARROW STANCE

90% WEIGHT FORWARD

Chip Shot: Backswing Position

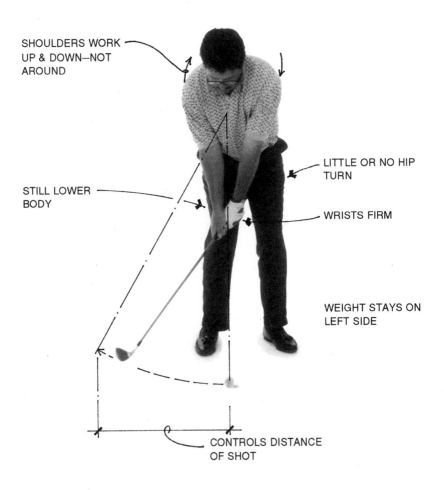

SHOULDERS WORK
UP & DOWN—NOT
AROUND

LITTLE OR NO HIP
TURN

STILL LOWER
BODY

WRISTS FIRM

WEIGHT STAYS ON
LEFT SIDE

CONTROLS DISTANCE
OF SHOT

Chip Shot: Impact Position

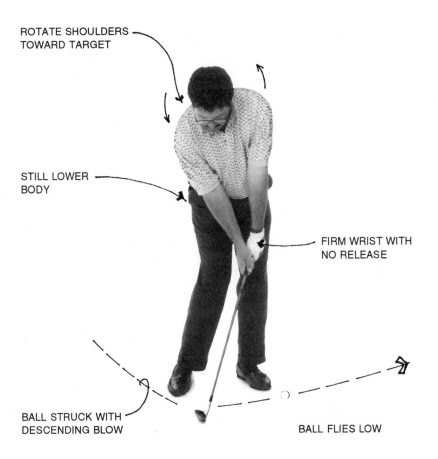

ROTATE SHOULDERS
TOWARD TARGET

STILL LOWER
BODY

FIRM WRIST WITH
NO RELEASE

BALL STRUCK WITH
DESCENDING BLOW

BALL FLIES LOW

Chip Shot: Finish Position

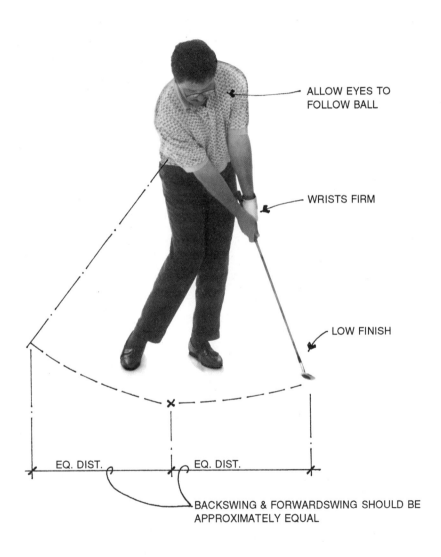

ALLOW EYES TO
FOLLOW BALL

WRISTS FIRM

LOW FINISH

EQ. DIST.   EQ. DIST.

BACKSWING & FORWARDSWING SHOULD BE
APPROXIMATELY EQUAL

PUTTING

There are more theories and techniques on putting than there are on the golf swing. The concept of putting is simple, *just roll the ball into the hole.* So why do golfers agonize over putts so much? Because putting can make or break the game. A golfer who's all over the fairway can salvage a good score if he or she can make putts, whereas a good ball striker hitting most greens in regulation will not score well if he or she can't make putts.

Putting is the easiest place to make up your score. Next time you play, keep track of your putts and see how you fare. A par round of golf will allow thirty-six putts or two putts per hole, therefore any improvement you make here will directly reflect on your score. If you lose a stroke out on the fairway, there is always a chance to make it up on the green. If you lose a stroke on the green, you can kiss it good-bye forever. I've seen many good players hit a great approach shot to the green only to three putt the hole, then leave absolutely disgusted. Many times this disgust carries over to the next hole and could carry on till the end of the round. To put it in perspective, you can be on the green in three on a 550-yard par 5, then walk away with a bogey because you three putted, or even worse. *Three shots to travel 545 yards, then three more shots to go 15 feet. Remember, a three-foot putt counts the same as a 300-yard drive; one stroke.*

Putting is also the most individualized aspect of the game. It is ninety percent mental. It requires relaxation, concentration and confidence. There's an endless quest to seek the divine knowledge that will make a great putter, and there is nothing about it written in stone. Putting is developed by *a feel for speed and distance, the ability to read the break,* and *the ability to adapt to playing conditions.* I think beginners worry too much about the break when they should be concentrating on the distance. Distance is the key for getting the putt down in two. If it goes in on one, it's a bonus.

Bear in mind that weather, temperature, time of day, time of season, how many golfers played the greens before you, the type of grass, when it was cut, and more will all affect the way the greens are played. All of those conditions, along with the knowledge and experience you have gained from playing, go into your brain to calculate the speed, distance and angle for your putt. The human brain is a marvel at learning and adjusting; it adapts to using any putter, grip or stance imaginable. When you go to the golf shop, take a look at how many different putters there are: center shafted putters, blade putters, long-shafted or short-shafted ones, some round, some flat, some shaped like a hot dog. Use whatever feels comfortable.

Watch the pros play and see how many grips you can find; some use a ten-finger grip, some an overlap grip, a reverse overlap grip, a split-handed grip; some putt cross handed, while others only use one hand. Use whatever you are comfortable using.

I have read multiple books, reviewed various tapes, cut out various magazine articles, and watched the pros to see if I could gain the secret technique. I found that there is no secret; putting is developed through experience and feel that is individual to each one of us. Tommy Armour summed it up when he said, "To become a good putter the main requisites are to keep the head dead still and make the putter blade go accurately toward the hole." [4]

There are no sure fire techniques to putting; there is no proper grip or stance to follow, nor are there any magical

---

4: Tommy Armour, <u>How to Play Your Best Golf All the Time</u> (Simon & Schuster, © 1953)

putters you can buy. The only physical requirement, is to possess a smooth and consistent stroke to start dropping putts. There are some basic techniques and thoughts that greatly improved my putting, and I believe they can help yours too.

PUTTING THOUGHTS

1. *Make the ball die at the hole:* I never liked the philosophy of never up, never in. Most beginners usually hit past the hole.

2. *Distance, distance, distance:* We worry too much about the break, distance is the key to getting down in two putts.

3. *Double the break:* Most beginners never play enough break; when you read the break, double it.

THE SETUP POSITION

A key point to remember for a putt is that you must get the ball *rolling* straight toward the hole. An ideal putting stroke strikes the ball at the equator causing it to slide forward a little before it starts rolling. This ensures the desired smooth roll in the direction you are aiming.

THE GRIP

The key to making a smooth and consistent stroke, is to minimize wrist action. I prefer the reverse overlap grip for putting as it is extremely effective for keeping the wrists very quiet. It places your entire right hand on the grip which is important for developing feel. It also lines up both hands on the ball for better control. The reverse overlap grip is similar to our regular grip. Instead of your right pinky over your left index finger, place all the fingers of your right hand on the club, and place the left index finger over the spot between the right pinky and ring fingers. This not only allows you to regulate the speed with your right arm, but helps prevent any unwanted cupping of the left wrist. Grip pressure should be very light.

THE STANCE

The feet are set in a narrow stance that is square with your weight slightly to the left. As you bend forward, place the ball directly opposite the left heel with your eyes directly over the ball. Hold the club so that a triangle is formed between your shoulders, arms, and the grip of your club. The shaft of the club should line up with your left leg, with your hands slightly behind the ball.

THE PUTTING STROKE

The putting stroke is similar to the chipping stroke as it works just like a pendulum. The club goes straight back and straight forward with no turning of the club. The shoulders work up and down as they rotate in a *linear motion,* not a circular one; as if you are rocking a baby. It is important to keep the wrists firm and the path of the backswing and downswing aligned down the target line. The lower body remains very still with no shifting of the weight. The length of the backswing should match the length of the follow-through as distance is controlled by the length of the backswing.

The idea is to strike the ball so that it slides forward first, then begins to roll. This ensures the proper rotation of the ball in the direction you are aiming. If the ball is struck with a descending blow, the backward spin acts like a brake throwing the ball off line. If the ball is struck under the equator, the ball bounces along the green. Playing the ball off your left foot virtually guarantees the ball being struck with a slightly ascending blow which produces the slight sliding action you are looking for.

The putting stroke is a true pendulum motion that does not move off the target line. The stroke does not accelerate; the tempo of the backswing and forwardswing are mirrors of each other. The back of the left hand and right palm should always be facing the target and the left wrist is kept firm. After the putt is struck, hold the finish, then turn your head well after the stroke is completed.

PUTTING KEY POINTS

Setup Position

1. Narrow stance with weight on balls of feet

2. 50 to 60 percent of your weight on the left side

3. Ball aligned inside the left heel, with eyes over ball

4. Reverse overlap grip with triangle between shoulders, arms and hands

5. Light grip pressure

Stroke

1. Rotate shoulders with a rocking motion in a linear, not circular, plane

2. Strike ball with an ascending blow as clubhead stays on target line

3. Head and lower body remain still

4. Keep head down until long after stroke

KEY THOUGHT

Distance, distance, distance

Putt: Setup Position

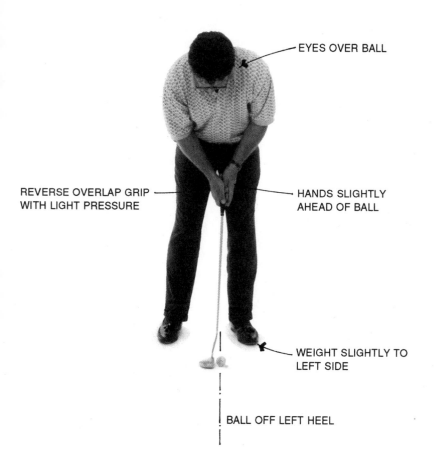

EYES OVER BALL

REVERSE OVERLAP GRIP
WITH LIGHT PRESSURE

HANDS SLIGHTLY
AHEAD OF BALL

WEIGHT SLIGHTLY TO
LEFT SIDE

BALL OFF LEFT HEEL

Putt: Backswing Position

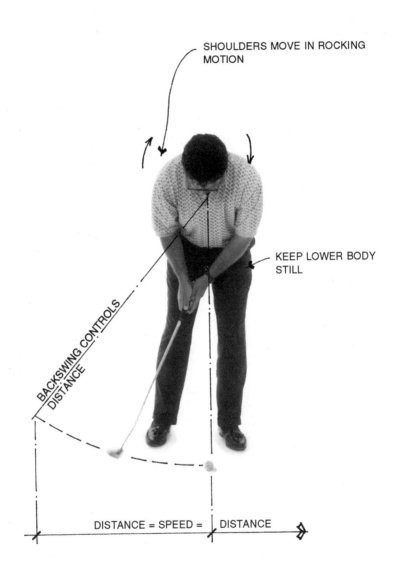

SHOULDERS MOVE IN ROCKING MOTION

KEEP LOWER BODY STILL

BACKSWING CONTROLS DISTANCE

DISTANCE = SPEED = DISTANCE

Putt: Impact Position

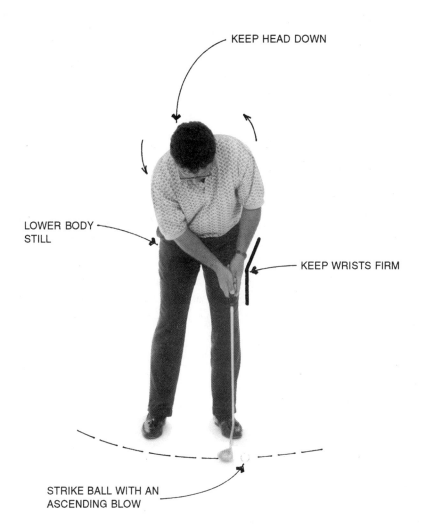

KEEP HEAD DOWN

LOWER BODY
STILL

KEEP WRISTS FIRM

STRIKE BALL WITH AN
ASCENDING BLOW

Putt: Finish Position

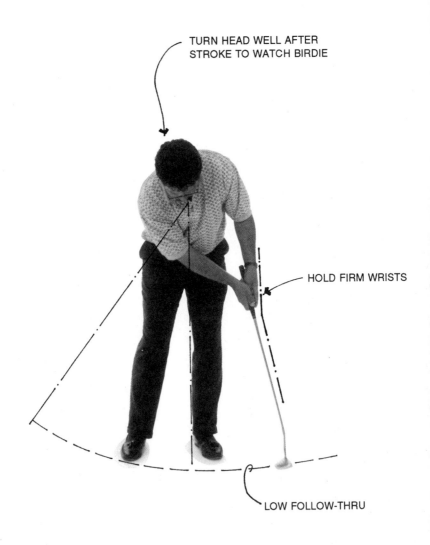

TURN HEAD WELL AFTER
STROKE TO WATCH BIRDIE

HOLD FIRM WRISTS

LOW FOLLOW-THRU

SMOOTH—SMOOTH—SMOOTH

CHAPTER SEVEN

PLAYING THE GAME
The Real Thing

Now that you've hit all those balls on the range, you're ready to have fun and play golf. Before taking lessons or receiving any instruction, most beginners have probably played golf at one time or another. It must have been an enjoyable experience if they are still playing and working toward getting better. There are a few guidelines that should be incorporated to make the game more enjoyable.

First, select the course you want to play, then call and reserve a tee time: *It's that simple!* You might ask about the dress code and if regulations allow you to walk the course. Some courses make it mandatory to take a golf cart. If you are a beginning golfer, don't select a course that is too difficult or it may become the longest day of your golfing life. The range of difficulty of golf courses are listed by course and slope ratings for each colored tee. Most golf courses have at least three different colored tees; many have four:

1. *Red tees:* Usually reserved for women players.

2. *Gold tees:* These tees can be played by anyone, but are mainly created for people who usually play white tees and are seeking a different perspective on the course. Also used by many 9-hole courses so players can play 18 by teeing off from the different colored tees for each 9 holes.

3. *White tees:* Designed for the middle-to high-handicap male player. By far the most used tee.

4. *Blue tees:* Usually reserved for tournament players or low-handicap players, but can be played by anyone seeking a different perspective on the same course.

Each colored tee on golf courses have a course rating and a slope rating. They are used to adjust handicaps and calculate the number of strokes each player will be allotted prior to play. Basically, the higher the ratings, the more difficult the course.

a. Course Rating: Generally means the score a scratch golfer would shoot playing his best in comparing all golf courses. This number can range anywhere from 60.0 to 75.0 with the higher number being a more difficult course.

b. Slope Rating: This number can range anywhere from 67 to 147. It is used to calculate the course handicap, or the number of strokes a player will receive on that particular course. To find the number of strokes, you simply multiply your handicap index by the slope rating of the golf course, divide by 113, then round to the nearest whole number. This is the number of strokes you should receive for this course.

If you are serious about golf and are interested in playing in local tournaments, you must get an established index or handicap. To do this, go down to your local golf course or a course you wish to designate as your home course, sign up and join their club. As you play, you post your scores after each round. Most courses have a computerized system where you simply punch in your membership number and score. It then records to your home club. After a certain number of rounds, you can go by your club and receive your index card. This card is constantly updated and reflects your current handicap over the last twenty games. It's a great way to measure your progress.

BEFORE YOU TEE OFF

You've been doing your stretches and your equipment is ready. The essential equipment is packed into your bag, along with any extraneous equipment you might need. You've selected the course, called your friends, and secured a tee time. *It's time to play!* The first thing you do is get mentally ready to play golf:

1. *Get to the course at least 20 minutes prior to your tee time:* Golf is best played when the mind and body are calm. It is impossible to be calm if you drive 100 mph to get to the course and sprint to the first tee while trying to put on your shoes. Give yourself some time to prepare. Hit some balls, do some putting, or perform a few simple stretches.

2. *Hit chips and putts if time is limited:* Many players like to hit a small bucket of balls before playing. If time is limited, it is far more productive to hit chips and putts. This will help develop some feel for the ball and the speed of the greens.

3. *Set your own par:* One of the best pieces of advice I ever received was from David Emerick, an instructor at the Golf University. During a round of golf, Dave told me to set my own par for the course and not try to shoot the course par. Par is a great score that a scratch golfer should shoot; to compare your game at this point to a scratch golfer is unrealistic. The Golf University came up with a personal scorecard that lets golfers set their own par. It also has a space to keep track of the good shots made during the round. The card works great for helping you make and attain realistic short term goals. When you look at a scorecard, you see holes like a 200-yard par 3, which is common on many courses. Keep in mind that all holes allow for two putts; for a beginner or high-handicapper to land the green with his tee shot and then get down in two is unrealistic. Most players would be very happy with a 4, so you should set your personal par to a 4. When you make a 4, you par the hole and achieve your goal. If you make a 3 (course par but a birdie for you), count it and celebrate the shot as a birdie. If you make a 5, you only bogeyed it.

GOLF UNIVERSITY SCORECARD

	HOLE	1	2	3	4	5	6	7	8	9	OUT	FRONT NINE SUMMARY
RESULTS	COURSE PAR											
	PERSONAL PAR											Praisings (What went well?)
	+ OR - YOUR PAR											
	Good Shots—Mark Each With A Plus Sign (+)											
REASONS	TEE SHOTS											
	FAIRWAY SHOTS											Redirections (What to do differently on the back nine?)
	SHORT SHOTS											
	PUTTS											
	SELF MANAGEMENT											

	HOLE	10	11	12	13	14	15	16	17	18	IN	TOTAL
RESULTS	COURSE PAR											
	PERSONAL PAR											
	+ OR - YOUR PAR											
	Good Shots—Mark Each With A Plus Sign (+)											
REASONS	TEE SHOTS											
	FAIRWAY SHOTS											
	SHORT SHOTS											
	PUTTS											
	SELF MANAGEMENT											

Of all the golfers I play with regularly, I don't know of one who has actually read the entire *Rules of Golf* published by the USGA. I've learned most of the general rules just by playing with experienced players. If I have a question, I ask someone or consult my rule book. There are some common courtesies that all players should adhere to that may *not be in any rule book:*

1. Call the pro shop if you can't make your tee time reservation and cancel it. Too many people fail to show up because of a conflict and forget to cancel. This is an inconvenience to the pro shop as well as other players who do not get to play because of no available tee times.

2. *Be quiet when someone is about to hit:* Sometimes the First and Tenth tees get crowded with players awaiting their turns. Try to give some consideration to other players on the tee. Talk between foursomes.

3. *Don't litter on the golf course:* Nothing is worse than discarded cans and wrappers strewn around a beautiful setting.

4. *Don't hit into a group waiting to play:* On weekends, the courses get busy and a round of golf could take over five hours. Bear in mind that the group ahead of you is probably waiting for the group ahead of them.

5. *Don't play slow!* While it is important to enjoy yourself with your friends in these beautiful settings, be courteous and don't hold other players up too long. Realize that one group can delay the entire day of play for each golfer who follows. If one person is hitting, others can be getting ready to hit. If two players are on opposite sides of the fairway, both can hit simultaneously without disrupting each other.

6. *Follow course rules:* On some par 3's, you might see a sign that reads: "When on the green, allow players behind to hit up." When your group is on the green and the group behind is waiting at the tee, mark your balls and let the group behind hit up. After they hit their tee shots, you can replace your balls and finish putting. Ideally, you want to finish before the other group arrives.

7. *Always rake the traps:* If you hit into a sandtrap, be sure to rake the trap smooth when you have finished. This is a potential problem on many courses.

8. *Replace divots:* After you've hit your shot, try to replace the grass or fill the divot with sand that is often supplied at the tees or on golf carts.

9. *Don't drag your feet on the greens:* Sometimes players get hot and tired and drag their feet; this tears up the greens so pick up your feet.

10.   *Fix ball marks:* When you get up to the greens, always repair your ball mark, then fix someone else's. You can nearly always find a ball mark that you didn't make but was not previously fixed.

PRE-SHOT ROUTINE

The pre-shot routine is probably the most important process a player can go through to mentally and physically prepare him or herself for making the shot. All good players have a consistent routine; poor players do not. By preparing yourself to hit the shot before you step up to the ball, you can eliminate the stray thoughts that creep into your head. Trying to reinvent your swing during a round of golf is a problem all amateurs have dealt with. How many times have you stood over the ball with a hundred different swing thoughts going through your head? This is very disruptive to the task at hand. All thinking should be done behind the ball. When you step up to the ball, the one and only thought you should have on your mind is the target. If you find this too difficult, take one swing thought with you to the tee such as *good weight shift, smooth takeaway, and so forth.* One simple thought won't hurt you, but keep it simple.

The key is developing a pre-shot routine that works for you. Some people are very visual; they need to picture the shot in their minds. Some are very kinetic; they need to get the feel for each shot. Others are auditory, they need to talk to themselves about the shot. The Golf University gave me a simple concept that helped me develop my pre-shot routine:

Tell yourself, show yourself, just do it!

Tell yourself: Stand behind the ball, feel the weight of the club, decide how you want to hit this shot, pick your target line. I like to pick a spot on the ground somewhere in front of the ball on the target line. This allows me to line up the clubhead on the ball as I am standing over the ball.

Show yourself: I like the way Corey Pavin does this; first, he makes a partial swing in slow motion that exaggerates what he is trying to do based on his swing thought. He then integrates that move into his full swing thus getting his rhythm and timing. I like to just feel the rhythm of the swing; when it feels good, I'm ready.

Just do it!: When you step up to the ball, you already know what you want to do. You already know how you are going to do it, so do it! When I'm ready, I quickly walk into the tee box, align my clubface on the ball with my aiming spot, then settle in with my stance. I get my feet settled, double check my target line, then relax my arms by letting them hang straight down. When I'm ready to swing, I waggle the club back and forth a little to keep my wrists loose. I take a deep breath, exhale, then let it rip.

The golfer's mind works in strange ways; you can have ten swing thoughts going through your mind in the time it takes you to swing the club. You must learn to focus your attention away from swing thoughts. This used to be a problem for me, but I substituted one phrase that wipes out all the other stray thoughts. I think:

Baackkkk . . . downnnn!

Your pre-shot routine will probably vary slightly for putting, chipping and pitching. In putting and chipping, you are trying to gage the speed; in pitching you are trying to gage distance; in the full swing you are gaging rhythm. The pre-shot routine controls every aspect of the swing. It takes tremendous discipline to apply it to every shot on the course. By having a set pre-shot routine, the mind is freed from thinking about the routine. The process is automatic. You can instead concentrate on the target and keep thinking to a minimum. Excess thinking causes unwanted tension, and tension results in bad golf swings.

COURSE MANAGEMENT

Play smart and don't try for impossible shots. How many times have you sliced your tee shot into a group of trees; pulled out a 3-wood and tried to blast the ball out of the rough between two trees under a low hanging limb and over another tree 100 yards down the fairway? We've all done it and some still do. What usually happens when you try that shot? If you get lucky, you make that shot and feel great. But four out of five times you probably hit another tree keeping you trapped in the woods. Eventually you get back to the fairway but by then you have dropped so many strokes you are lucky to get on the green in par. A smart play would have been to pitch out from the trees to the fairway to set up your third shot. You lose a stroke, but still have a good chance for par if you hit it close. Example:

You come to a par 5, 500-yard hole; player one hits a 250-yard drive, a 200-yard second shot, pitch on the green, then 2 putts for a par 5. Player two slices his drive 200-yards into the trees, pitches back to the fairway, hits a 200-yard third shot, pitch on the green close, and 1 putts for a par 5. You will always have a chance to make up strokes lost on the fairway with a good short game. If you hit an errant drive, there is no need to panic. If you were playing a match and this was the last hole, you may have no choice but to try a low percentage shot. But for most games, it's better to play smart.

Play your clubs with feeling and intuition. Just because you're 100 yards out, doesn't mean you only use your 100-yard club. I hit a full-pitching wedge around 100 yards, but many times I can achieve the same result using an 8-iron with a three-quarter swing. When you hit your clubs fairly consistently and develop a feel for distance, try taking one-half or three-quarter swings. See what happens to the ball. Notice how the flight of the ball varies with the strength of your swing. On a very loose and relaxed swing, the ball flies on a high trajectory. If you hit the ball with a more deliberate swing, the ball flies lower. If your ball ends up under a tree, you'll need that lower controlled punch shot. It is just a matter of how you want to hit the shot. You are the best judge of your own skills and should maximize your abilities.

Good course management comes from experience and common sense. Here are some simple thoughts that will help keep your game more manageable and lower your scores.

1. *Play within yourself:*   Know your limitations.   If you've never hit a bump and run shot, the course is not the place to try it. Only hit shots that you have previously practiced and have confidence in.

2. *Don't correct your swing during a round:*   If you're hitting a fade, play the fade; if you're hitting a draw, play the draw. Work on correcting your swing later at the range. As Sam Snead said: "Yuh gotta dance with who yuh brung."

3. *Hit away from trouble:*   If there is water on the right side of the fairway, tee the ball on the right side of the box and hit to the left. Even if you pull your ball into some trees or another fairway, you will still be in bounds with no penalties.

4. *Don't be short:*   Almost all amateur players miss greens because they hit short. Just because you hit a 6-iron 160 yards at the range doesn't mean you are going to do it on the course. Remember, at the range you have perfect lies, hard durable balls that don't cut and fly far, and you can swing hard because you don't need to worry about staying in the fairway. It's better to take a longer club and swing easy.

5. *Stay in the present:*   If you hit a bad shot, forget about it. Don't carry it with you.   What happens with a lot of players is that they will try too hard on the next shot to make up for the last one, causing another bad shot. At the same token, don't celebrate until the job is finished. Never anticipate results. If you do, you will lose focus on the task at hand.

6. *Play clubs you are confident in:*   If you are not confident with your driver, don't use it. Tee off with a club you can hit. A friend of mine uses his 8-iron on anything from 120

yards to 170 yards. He has confidence with that club and can make it perform how he wants it to. We call it his *Magic 8*.

7. *Don't say don't:* Ken Blanchard said, "The mind does not recognize the word don't." When you say "don't hit in the sandtrap," you really mean hit in the sandtrap. When hitting over a hazard, try to pretend the hazard is not there. Too many times we over-emphasize trouble and give the shot a *little extra* in an effort to clear the hazard. Sometimes the extra effort gets our hands too involved which may lead to sculling or topping the shot into the hazard. Extra effort can also sail the ball over the hazard, then over the green and into another hazard. Just make your normal swing.

8. *Play your favorite club for the approach shot.* Most amateurs on par 5's hit a driver off the tee, then a 3-wood for their second shot. Rethink that second shot. Most player's can't get on the green in two, so the third shot can be anything from a full 5-iron to a short pitch with a wedge. *Play your best club as your approach shot.* If you have a lot of confidence in your pitching wedge and hit it 100 yards consistently, your second shot should end up 100 yards out from the pin. This allows you to hit your best short iron into the green.

Good course management might not be spectacular, but it will shave strokes off your game.

CHAPTER EIGHT

HOW TO PRACTICE
It's Not Exercise

Practice is a word that no one gets excited about or looks forward to. But to improve at anything, it takes practice. Most golfers don't practice properly; they do what everybody else does and hit buckets of balls.

The next time you go to the range, observe how many people dump the bucket of balls next to them and continually rake balls in, hit—rake a ball, hit—rake a ball, hit. They always start with a 9-iron, bang away a dozen balls, then switch clubs and bang away with an 8-iron, then switch clubs again. Eventually they pull out the driver. After hitting a few slices, they make the most awkward stances and adjustments to their grips and stances in an effort to hit the ball straight. This reminds me of my friend Tony. He will hit 200 balls before I finish my bucket of 80. I love watching him rake balls in and blast away, rake another ball in and blast away, most of the time never breaking his grip. He always finishes the same way; picking at his blisters while he mumbles something about taking more lessons. This will not help your game. *This is not practice, this is exercise!*

Occasionally, players go over and practice chips and putts, but 90 per cent of their time is devoted to practicing the full swing. The next time you play, keep track of all your shots; full swings, pitches, chips and putts. If you analyze a typical round of golf, you will find the full swing only accounts for about thirty-seven percent of your score, while sixty-three per cent of your shots will be pitches, chips and putts. A scratch round of golf is calculated with thirty-six putts or half the total score.. A sure-fire way to drop strokes off your score is to concentrate on practicing your short game.

HOW TO PRACTICE

Upon my arrival at the Golf University, located at the beautiful Ranch Bernardo Inn in Rancho Bernardo, California, I was excited to start the four-day course. I arrived Sunday evening and was treated to an exceptional meal at the El Bizcocho Restaurant. Over dinner Dave Witt, an instructor at the Golf University, gave me some great advice on how to practice. He said the one greatest flaw most beginners have is that they work too hard on trying to hit the ball before they develop good swing mechanics. Trying too hard to hit the ball makes you cast your arms and hands at the ball producing very inconsistent shotmaking. You should swing through the ball and not hit it; it's the swinging motion that's important. *The best way I have found to remember this is: Just swing the club, the ball happens to get in the way.*

Dave stressed the importance of first developing the swing before worrying about hitting the ball. Once good swing mechanics are in place, then you can concentrate on other aspects of good ball-striking. Dave gave me four steps to follow for developing a good swing:

1. *Swing:* Practice your swing 60 times a day for 21 straight days. Don't hit a ball and don't worry about a target. Your goal is to feel the swing and have confidence in it.

2. *Contact:* After the 21 days, go to the range. Pick a club that you don't like to hit and try for five centered shots. Don't worry about the swing since you should not be thinking about it at this point anyway. To verify that you strike the ball in the center of the clubface, use contact tape which can be purchased at most golf shops. This tape leaves an impression where the ball contacts the clubface. After you have hit at least five centered shots, leave the range.

3. *Target:* Go to the range and this time concentrate on a target. You already know that you are swinging the club well if you are contacting the center of the clubface, so your only thought should be on the target.

4. *Goal setting:* Set realistic goals for yourself when you are practicing. Once you attain the goals, praise yourself and leave. The words *"achieve and leave"* will give you satisfaction and a sense of accomplishment during your practice sessions. Don't worry about the balls you leave behind. Someone will use them. Always finish your practice on a good shot; never end on a bad one.

In ideal practice situations, it is important to approach each shot as if it were on a golf course. If time allows, go through your pre-shot routine. Set-up to the ball and strike the ball. Praise yourself if you are successful and redirect yourself if you are not. While it may not be practical to go through your full pre-shot routine on every ball you hit, try to imagine you are hitting these shots on a golf course and not just repetitively hitting the same shots. One suggestion is to go through the full pre-shot routine on every fourth or fifth ball you hit. This keeps the routine from getting monotonous. Never allow yourself to rush your pre-shot routine in an effort to hit balls as this will only carry over to the course.

One successful method of practice is to pretend you are playing a round of golf. Take a scorecard and play every hole as you would on the actual course. If you hit an errant shot, play your next shot like you would on the course. If you sliced your drive off, take a wedge and pitch it to the center. Before I learned to hit the ball straight, I was always among the trees on the right side of the fairway. From this position, I learned that low punch and run shot under tree limbs. It is a great shot to practice at the range and can pay dividends on the course. Also, try some high lob shots over an imaginary tree. With a little imagination, you can play a round of golf and never leave the practice tee. Obviously, you can skip the putter on the practice tee. After you're done on the tee, go over to the putting green and sink a few birdies.

PUTTING PRACTICE

First, you should practice like you play. No one plays with three or four balls or takes numerous putts at the same hole from the same distance. Use only one ball to practice your putts; you are trying to duplicate game conditions. Set some goals for your practice session and when you achieve them, move on to something else. A good example might be:

1. Make a 5 foot putt, three times

2. Two putt from 25 feet, three times

3. Two putt from 50 feet, three times

When you practice these, hit them in rotation and continue that way until each distance is completed. Hit one 5 footer, than make two putts for the 25 footer, than the 50 footer, then start back at the 5 footer. After each distance putts are completed, that distance can be skipped until your goals are completed. You may make all the 5 footers and 25 footers before you make any 50 footers. At this point, you would keep shooting 50 footers until your task is completed.

CHIPPING PRACTICE

As the putting practice goes, so does the chipping practice. Take one ball and set some goals for your chipping practice. Achieve them and leave. A good example might be:

1. Pick a short target (15 feet or so) and chip a ball within 2 feet, three times

2. Pick a long target (40 feet or so) and chip a ball within 4 feet, three times

You can try different clubs depending on how much green you have to work with and how much fringe you have to clear. Get to know how each club can work for you.

PITCHING PRACTICE

For pitching practice, I don't expect you to use one ball as it wouldn't be practical. Again, set varying targets usually one short and one long, and the goals you have for each. Practice some pitching variations; high lob shots and pitch and run shots. When you're on the course, you may need some of these shots. A good example would be:

1. Short target (30 yards); pitch 3 balls within 6 feet of flag

2. Long target (60 yards); pitch 3 balls on the green. You may need to decide on the boundary of the green if one does not exist.

SAND PRACTICE

Again, use multiple balls. Try different positions in the trap with different lies. Try a buried lie shot or a shot close to the edge of the trap. When you set the ball a little back in the stance, the ball comes out lower and longer.

1. Short target (adjacent green); pitch 3 balls on to the green

2. Long target (40 yards); pitch 3 balls on the green

FULL SWING PRACTICE

1. Decide what you want to work on here. If you performed well in the other practice sessions, you have plenty of balls left to practice your drives. If you have twenty balls left, you may just want to hit four good drives. If you have fifty balls left, you might hit four good drives, and six good fairway shots with your other woods. The key is to achieve your goals and leave. Never end on a bad shot; always finish with a good shot, even if you have twenty balls left.

There will be many times that you only feel like practicing the full swing; it is the most fun. If you're going to hit a bucket of balls, vary your clubs often. Don't systematically start with your 9-iron, then work up to your driver. You don't play the course like that, so why should you practice that way.

Try hitting only your wedges sometime. Proficiency with your wedges at the range will carry over to the productivity of your game on the course.

Also, put extra practice in clubs you don't like to hit. It's easy to practice with your favorite club; you always seem to hit it great. But at the range, are you really trying to impress anyone around you? When you hit a bad shot on the range, it doesn't count against you whereas on the course, it does.

TAKING LESSONS:

I can't stress the importance of taking proper lessons. Taking a few lessons from a competent instructor will not only help your game, but make it more enjoyable. My instructor Jim Perez, is a USGTF certified teaching pro who teaches at the Islewood Golf Range in Fresno, California. Jim gave me simple drills that enabled me to feel the proper swing. Some players are audible; they need to hear how to do the proper swing. Some are very visual; they need to see the proper swing. I'm a very tactile person; I need to feel the proper swing. Once I feel the swing, it is easy to duplicate it on the course.

It is also important to have your instructor videotape your swing. Golf is a difficult sport to become proficient at; when you can view yourself on the screen, your faults become very apparent. In this way, it is easy to identify and correct the swing faults.

CHAPTER NINE

SWING THOUGHTS
A Mental Approach

Why do we play golf? Are we trying to make a living at it, or are we just trying to have some fun? Ninety-nine percent of golfers play it for fun and recreation. So why do they get angry and frustrated when they're not playing well? Many players take the game too seriously. They are more concerned with their score than having a good time; they mentally beat themselves up when not playing well. This carries over into the physical part of their game. Being frustrated and angry only tenses your body making it more difficult to make a good golf swing. It's just a matter of time before the errant shots keep multiplying and your frustration level grows higher. At this point: *The harder you try, the worse you are bound to do!*

It has been said that golf is ninety percent mental and ten per cent physical. How do you feel when you finish a round of golf? Are you mentally and physically drained, or do you feel refreshed and energized? If you don't feel like the latter, you need to change your perspective on the game.

There always seems to be someone in the group that is whining and complaining about everything. If he or she is not playing well, it's the course conditions, or it's the weather, or it's the clubs. Playing with this type of golfer generally ruins the day for everyone. These are ones I avoid playing with. They mentally beat themselves up on the course bringing you down with them.

When I attended the Golf University, one of the keys stressed was mental attitude. Ken Blanchard, founder of the Golf University, and who is best known for his management skill in business, wrote a book called *Playing the Great Game of Golf, Making Every Minute Count*. In his book, he applies his wisdom and knowledge to playing golf. Having read it, I became more aware of why I was playing golf, and how to keep a positive attitude during the progression of my game. I learned to stop beating myself up when I hit a bad shot, and found something good about every shot I hit on the course. I set realistic goals for myself, like setting my own par (it's unrealistic for you to shoot par unless you're a par golfer). When my goals were achieved, I found a great sense of accomplishment which further motivated me. So don't concern yourself with just how far you drove the ball, or how many strokes over par you are. *Play the game as it was intended; it's only a game and we play games to better enjoy life.*

WHY DO YOU PLAY GOLF?

The first thing you have to do is figure out why you play golf. I play golf to have fun; after a hard week of work, I need to unwind. I enjoy the scenery; golf courses can have some of the most beautiful settings, even in an urban environment. I enjoy the company of my friends; any activity you participate in will be enjoyable if you're doing it with good friends.

Golf is fun: Remember, you are playing golf to relax, so relax and have fun! If you're like most golfers, you work hard all week and want to unwind on the weekends. I can't think of a more relaxing day then to spend some time with my friends playing a great game in some of the most beautiful settings around. Whether the fun is getting your first birdie or hitting a monster drive that stayed in the fairway, or playing a round with the same ball. Just spending time with friends is good enough for me. The fact is; you *choose* to be on the golf course and you *choose* to play golf. Since this is not work it must be play, and we play to have fun.

Some of the best times I've had on a golf course have been watching the unbelievable shots my friends make; and I don't mean good, but unbelievable. Recently I was playing with some good friends—Brian, Sean and Tony. In fairness to Brian, he just started playing and is not interested in taking lessons. It was on a par 4, 400-yard hole and Brian was the first to tee. He teed the ball, then took one of those big self-taught swings that he picked up playing baseball. The ball took off on a 90-degree angle from the tee defying all known laws of physics. It hit the ball washer and came directly at us. Luckily, no one was hurt as we are all pretty agile and dove out of the way. After the usual ribbing, we told Brian to tee up another ball and hit again. This time, we stood behind the tee box so it would be impossible to get hit by the ball. To this day, I can honestly say the odds for his next shot are far longer than Ed McMahon showing up at your doorstep with a ten million dollar check. He hit the ball solid and it took off like a shot. It then hit the women's tee marker square twenty yards away, came straight back over our heads and settled 25 yards behind us. We laughed so hard we could hardly settle down to hit our own shots.

The point is, we all had fun with it and could laugh about it, even Brian. The score wasn't that important to us. I think we were playing for a round of beers. We were playing to be with friends, to spend some time together talking and laughing. I think it's important to play with people who don't take themselves too seriously. If you don't have fun playing, then you need to figure out why you are doing it.

DON'T CHEAT YOURSELF

Golf is a game founded on honesty, but in reality it has more habitual cheating than any other sport. Golf is probably the only professional sport in which competitors police themselves. They are expected to, and they often call penalties and infractions upon themselves. Too many players over emphasize the importance of score. I read somewhere that the average score for a man is around 92 and a woman around 102. I would bet that if golfers played by USGA rules, most would not break 100. I've seen many serious golfers that are very competitive *cheat*. It seems that they're so hung up on their scores and handicaps, posting a score higher than they think they should be shooting becomes a lesson in humility. They either post what they should have shot or don't post anything at all. During play they also improve the position of their balls on the course. It may involve moving their ball out of a divot to a nice piece of grass, or moving their ball away from a tree. According to rule 13-2, a player cannot improve the lie of their ball except as provided by the rules. I think beginner's especially put too much emphasis on the score, and not enough importance on making good shots. Players posting scores in these *improved lie* rounds, are hurting themselves by posting scores that give them a handicap index not indicative of the way they are truly capable of playing. The competitive ego gives importance to the score: *a measure of our abilities.* This not only hurts you in a tournament, but gives you a false skill level. In a tournament, strict rules of golf are generally enforced, not the modified ones that you and your buddies play by. If you enter a tournament with an index of ten, you should shoot around 82. When you come into the clubhouse with a 92, you feel that you not only let yourself down, but you let your team down. If your index was truly reflective of your game, your 92 would probably help your team, and your self-esteem would be boosted.

When playing a friendly game with friends, there are usually a lot of mulligans, gimmes, and adjustments to the lie and position of the ball. You should be aware of how this affects your future in organized tournaments:

1. Your progress cannot be accurately recorded; there are no formulas for factoring in gimmes. To get a true measure and accurately calculate how many strokes you will receive for any given course, count every stroke.

2. It gives you a false handicap index. If you sign up for a scramble event or your club tournament, you already have given away all the strokes you didn't count previously.

3. Even in a friendly game, how can you determine who wins if everyone is cheating?

To get a true measure of your index, here are a couple of suggestions to follow:

- *Don't improve your lies:* I have seen many players dig their ball out from under a lip in a sandtrap, pull their ball out of a divot or deep rough, kick their ball out from under a tree to the fairway, and move their ball if a tree is blocking the target. If you're not keeping score, then it's okay to improve your lie if you're just practicing shots. I move my ball if the lie risks damage to my club during a swing; if the ball is by a rock or tree root. *Damaging my club or hurting myself is not worth avoiding the rule violation.*

- *Sink every putt:* Practice those one to two footers; give yourself confidence when you really need it. How often have you putted from around 30 feet out, got it within a couple of feet, then your buddy says *that's good.* What do you think when you hear that? I always picked up my ball with a sense of relief, that I didn't have to make that short little putt. If I got it close from a long way out, it gave me the right to give myself an automatic. But I was really hurting myself. I was so caught up in trying to get a good score, I avoided the extra pressure of making that short putt. When you play in tournaments, or friendly competition with friends, you need to make those short putts. An 8-inch putt counts the same as a 300-yard drive, *one stroke.*

The handicap system was designed to let players of different calibers compete against one another. Your handicap is your personal record of how your game is progressing, so don't cheat yourself. Be honest.

BAD LUCK AND GOOD LUCK BALANCE OUT

This past summer, I played at Chalk Mountain in Atascadero, California. The tenth hole was a 512-yard downhill par 5 that I hit a monster drive on. I then took my 3-wood and hit a great looking shot that headed for the green; *I was already planning my eagle putt.*   When the ball hit just short of the green, it should have rolled up onto the green. But it didn't. Instead the ball took a wicked sideways bounce and ended up behind a tree sitting in some deep rough. It must have hit something, possibly a sprinkler head or pine cone. Instead of the possible eagle putt, I found myself scrambling trying to salvage bogey; I made a seven. I could have let this bad luck ruin my game, but I remembered something I learned from Ken Blanchard—*Play in the present.*   In other words, don't dwell on the past or play in the future, keep the focus of your game in the present. I still had eight more holes to play.

I bogeyed the eleventh hole which was okay for me. Bogey on that hole was my personal par. The twelfth hole is a 176-yard par three that set up well for my slight fade. This is usually a 4-iron for me but I was hitting a little short that day, so I thought I would swing my 3-iron *easy.* I pulled out my 3-iron and aimed left knowing that I usually fade my long irons. When I hit the ball, I knew instantly I was in trouble. Of course, my easy swing developed more clubhead speed than I intended and I hit it square. My easy swing also relaxed my arms which allowed the club to turn over. All of a sudden, my 176-yard fade shot turned into a 200-yard draw heading left and long, over the green. This ball would surely have gone out and been lost in the bushes if it had not hit a tree. It ricocheted off the tree about midway up the trunk. With a resounding "whack" it bounced off the tree, landed on the green and ended up about three feet from the cup. *I made a birdie.*

Luck has a way of balancing itself out. Don't despair if you get unlucky. Just realize that what goes around comes around and luck will come your way.

ACCEPT COMPLIMENTS

Learn to pat yourself on the back; praise yourself on all the goals you reach on the golf course. Recognize your accomplishments as being goals achieved, and continue to set higher goals. Find something good about every shot you hit and don't dwell on the bad ones.

One guy I used to play with was a big whiner, always complaining and cussing every time he hit an errant shot, which became more frequent as his frustration grew. He was a very serious golfer who played to a legitimate sixteen handicap. Occasionally, he would hit a great shot but never seemed to feel it was good enough. There was a 406-yard par 4 in which he hit his drive about 230-yards right down the middle of the fairway; not good enough for his standards. He pulled out a 4-iron, hit the ball and landed it in the middle of the green fifteen feet to the left of the pin. *Great shot!* I exclaimed. He replied, *Damn! I pulled it left!*

Praise is important for our confidence and self-esteem. When someone gives praise or encouragement, you should accept it and build on it. When you hit a great shot, realize that you are capable of hitting great shots. If someone in your group makes a good shot, let him or her know with a simple acknowledgement. If you hit a great shot and no one acknowledges it, praise yourself and carry that positive energy with you.

I played with my brother-in-law Greg one summer. We played with two of his friends who were both single-digit handicappers. Greg was a beginner and I was in my second year of playing. My game was nowhere near single digits, but I steadily improved every time I went out. The two single-digit players had their own little competition going. Greg and I were just having fun. I hit the ball exceptionally well that day, and had recently purchased a new driver. Up until then, I was not yet confident with my driver, so I left it in the bag. I had been teeing off with my 3-wood and actually hitting the ball with a draw instead of my usual fade. We then got to the sixteenth hole which was a 396-yard par 4. Everyone hit; Greg was off in the trees and his two friends were down the fairway 240 and 250 yards respectively. I thought what the hell, I'm going to hit my driver. I was a little tentative about swinging it too hard as my earlier trial runs produced big slices. Nonetheless, I felt like I was swinging the club really well that day so I wanted to give it a shot. I teed the ball low, then took a nice easy swing and connected. What happened next was unbelievable. As soon as I hit the ball, I knew I hit it right on the screws and it was going long. It had that low trajectory that steadily climbs as it sails straight down the fairway. *Great shot Dave!* exclaimed Greg. I could hardly believe it myself. I had never hit a shot with such power, so I just stood there watching it go. I looked over at his two buddies who didn't say a word since they were already walking up the fairway. I felt cheated. Being a fairly new player, I wanted that positive reinforcement from my peers; at least Greg gave me some. I also patted myself on the back as I walked by the other two guys lining up their second shots. After I got to my ball some sixty yards past where theirs ended, I took my pitching wedge, and put the ball close to the pin. Unfortunately, I *missed* my birdie putt. ***Oh well, way to go on a great drive!***

SET YOUR OWN GOALS

Setting realistic and achievable goals is very important to the progress of your game. Your goals need to be specific, not general. Just saying, *my goal is to play well today,* is not a real measurable goal. It is better to say, *I've been swinging the club pretty well lately, I would be ecstatic with an 84.* By the end of the day, you can look at your scorecard, and say; *I played pretty well; I was only two over my goal,* or hopefully you will say; *I played great! I shot two under my goal and hit great drives all day!* By setting and achieving your goals, you will be giving yourself positive reinforcement and also build confidence in your abilities. When I started karate, my ultimate goal was a black belt. But my short-term goals were the belts in between. Golf goals should be the same. Your long-range goal might be to play scratch, but your short-term goal might be to break 100. When I first started playing, my immediate goal was to hit good shots. I didn't care or want to know what my scores were.

After setting a goal, it is important to write it down. When you achieve it, feel good and praise yourself for achieving it. Know that you have accomplished something you set out to do, and can accomplish anything you set your mind to. Then reset your goals, write them down and work toward attaining them. Your goal might be as simple as playing a round and having a couple of beers and a nice lunch with your friends. Or it may be as high as to play on a pro tour; whatever it is, make it achievable. Once you set that goal, have a plan for achieving it. If you're a beginning golfer and your goal is to play scratch, set your short-term goals in realistic and attainable increments. They might look like this:

Immediate goals:

a. To keep the ball in the fairway

b. Play with only one ball

Short term goals:

a. Break 100 within the next six months

b. Beat my buddy golfing

c. Shoot my first birdie (1 under par on one hole)

Long term goal:

a. To obtain a handicap of one or lower

DR. JEKYLL AND MR. HYDE

Golf is a great measure of character flaws. Playing a round of golf with someone shows what the person is made of. Does he or she whine and complain, cheat to win, make excuses for poor performances, throw tantrums? Is he or she a good loser, a gracious winner? Playing a round of golf with someone you know or think you know reveals character flaws, and presents the true individual.

SMELL THE ROSES

The fast-paced world in which we live gears us to perform tasks in an expedient manner. We tend to focus on the task at hand, and wear blinders to the environment around us. I'll be the first to admit that when I'm at work and someone speaks to me about non-work related topics, my attention span wanes and I want to get back to what I was doing. I have even been known to walk away in the middle of a conversation, not realizing what I was doing. I was just too focused and single-minded to listen to what people were saying. I've made a conscious effort to fix this problem, and hopefully now I am better.

Many people play golf too single-mindedly and focus only on their scoring. They miss everything around them; the relaxed pace, good conversation, breath-taking scenery. My first visit to Pebble Beach last summer made me realize how beautiful golf courses can be. I drove there with a friend on one of those get-out-of-town-to-unwind trips. We are both golf enthusiasts, but had no intention of playing that day. We just wanted to enjoy the scenery. After arriving, we parked the car and immediately walked over to the famed eighteenth hole, a place we had seen only on tv. It was more beautiful than I pictured, a 548-yard par 5 that wrapped along the cliffs overlooking the Pacific Ocean. The sun was out, the waves were crashing as the soft sea breezes caressed your senses. We sat down on the grass, and watched people play. There were an abundance of tourists shuffling through taking pictures around the eighteenth green. Pebble Beach is a beautiful golf course and I long to play there, but it is expensive at $225 per round. It is also a tough course and it intimidated me. With a slope rating of 138 off the white tees, I felt I wasn't ready to play the course. I began to think back as to why I became a golfer. As I watched, there were two types of players that came through, *serious and fun. It was very clear to me that day which group I wanted to be part of.*

Serious groups: You don't have to be a good golfer to play the Pebble Beach course. After watching about six groups play through, I would guess that most of these players couldn't break 100. Of the first group we watched, two out of four players almost broke windows of the houses that line the fairways to the right. The second group basically rolled their balls down the fairway taking seven or eight shots to reach the green. The group after them were a bunch of loud cigar-smoking guys that chewed out some tourist for taking pictures while they were teeing off. Those players were betting against each other, and I guessed much of that bet was riding on this last hole. Three out of the four missed the fairway and ended up in the rough. As we walked back down the cart path toward the green, I saw one of them kick his ball out from behind a tree in the rough to the fairway when his buddies weren't looking.

The problem was they weren't enjoying themselves. Every group except one were in golf carts. They would drive up to the ball, jump out and grab a club, hit the ball, and then immediately jump in the cart and race to the next ball. I didn't see many groups talking much amongst themselves, other than the cigar smoking group. Nor did I see smiles on many of their faces. They were so caught up in their scores, they missed many of the reasons they started playing golf. Here we are at one of the most beautiful courses on the planet, and nobody seems to be enjoying the big picture.

None seemed to be enjoying the scenery! I think golf carts have a lot to do with that. People drive carts like they drive cars; they concentrate on the road and not their surroundings. That is great—essential for driving your car—you do need to concentrate on the road. But when playing golf, you should enjoy the surrounding scenery, the company of friends, and the challenge of the course.

Fun groups: The only group taking advantage of their situation was the group that was walking. They were walking and laughing with the caddy. They walked along the cliffs looking at the views and made pleasant conversation while walking down the fairway; they were congratulating one another on their good shots. This group not only possessed the best players (three of the four hit the green in regulation), but they seemed to be having the best time.

Friendly competition is a lot of fun between friends. I always play better when I am playing for something; a skins game for a nickel a hole, or a $2 Nausau ($2 per each nine holes, then for the 18 hole total), or for beers, which generally costs more than any of the aforementioned games. Ken Blanchard, in his book, *Playing the Great Game of Golf,* tells a great story about a wealthy man who suggested a $2 Nausau to his foursome at the club. One of the new members, a young hotshot said, *Let's make it worth our while and play for $10.* The wealthy man responded, *If it's too low, let's play for $500.* The hotshot was taken back and said, *I can't afford $500.* The wealthy man responded, *Well I can, so let's play for $2.*

The point is that competition among friends is friendly; the prize that you are playing for is irrelevant. Don't allow the prize to blind you.   While I think it is important to concentrate and focus on your shots, don't let that focus disrupt your purpose for playing golf.   You can play any course around the world and enjoy yourself; you don't have to be intimidated by any course.   The mystique of Pebble Beach made me think it was like one of those double-black diamond runs on the ski slopes (for experts only!).   In reality, anyone that wanted to play could play and enjoy themselves.   I suddenly wished that I had brought my clubs with me.

FIND SOME GOOD IN EVERY SHOT

Accentuate the positive and don't dwell on the negative.   If you hit a bad shot, let it go.   When you hit a good shot, enjoy it and store it.   By not dwelling on your mistakes, the positive energy you get from a great shot will carry over into all phases of your game as well as your life.   I was playing with some friends out at Fig Garden Golf Course in Fresno.   We got to the ninth hole which was a 301-yard par 4.   A $2 Nausau was riding on this hole so the tension was in the air.   My buddies all hit pretty good tee shots, around 200 to 220 yards down the middle of the fairway.   I pulled out my driver thinking I could imitate John Daly and drive the green.   I completely over-swung the club forgetting everything I've learned and proceeded to top the ball.   I watched it roll down the fairway some 100 yards from the tee box.   I didn't let it get to me nor did I get mad for trying such a dumb shot.   I looked at my friends and said, *Well, at least I hit it straight!*

By not dwelling on my poor shot, and not thinking that I just threw away the $2, I completely forgot about the shot by the time I reached my ball.   Since I was playing in the present and not in the past, I pulled out my 5-wood, took a nice easy swing, and dropped the ball on the green. I won the $2 after I drained my birdie putt. The point is, concentrate on the task at hand. Don't worry about what happened before and don't try to anticipate what is going to happen. Play each shot in the present and try to remain positive.

DON'T SAY "DON'T!"

As mentioned before, saying "Don't hit it in the trap," or "Don't hit it in the water," almost guarantees you doing just that. Don't concentrate on the obstacle, just pretend it isn't there.   Make your shot as if the obstacle does not exist. Emphasizing the problem makes you alter your normal shot by using your arms and hands. This will likely make you hit a fat or thin shot, putting your ball where you did not want it to go. Before you step up to the ball, get into your pre-shot routine gaining a feel for the shot. When you are ready to hit the ball, step up to the ball, focus on the target, then make your normal swing.

Remember, bunkers and water hazards are merely visual barriers. *Don't make them mental blocks.*

FIRST TEE JITTERS

All golfers experience first tee jitters.   It's early Sunday morning. You think you should be in church but you're on the first tee. You're not that confident in your swing; you haven't had time to relax after racing to make your tee time; a dozen or so other players are waiting behind your group. You feel like you are teeing off on the 72nd hole of the U.S. Open, and everyone is watching. Some say playing golf is like being in church. *Oh please God, just let me hit the ball!*

First, realize that you have practiced for countless hours, have put time in at the range and hit many great shots. You should be fairly confident with your swing, so just make your normal swing. Do not:

- Try to kill the ball in an effort to impress everyone with your distance

- Rush your pre-shot routine in an effort to get off the tee

- Carry a hundred swing thoughts in your head

Realize that everyone gets a little nervous on the first tee. As your confidence grows, your jitters begin to go away. Get your round off to a good start. Do:

- Go through your normal complete pre-shot routine with no shortcuts

- Put the ball in play; don't concern yourself with distance, that will come naturally

- Carry one swing thought; it is unrealistic to shut out all thoughts on the first tee, especially for a beginner

- Take a deep breath and relax

Golf is a funny game; one day you're on, and one day you're not. Some days you're great off the tee, only to have your short game fall apart. Other days you can't seem to hit a fairway but your putter suddenly grows hot. Just when you think you have it figured out, the game quickly brings you back to reality. Even if you've had absolutely the worst day of golf in your life, realize that tomorrow is a whole new day. Even the pros have their good days and bad. Most of them spend thousands of dollars on sports psychologists to be told just that. It's a game of extreme emotions, from jubilation and excitement to frustration and despair. Golf works the intellect as well as the emotions. The intellect absorbs information from instructors, videos, books, and any sources available. It processes this information, takes it to the practice range, and learns from it by trial and error. This is the learning process that makes players better. The emotional part keeps golfers coming back time and time again to enjoy the highs golf gives us. Built-in egos keep the good shots and forget most of the bad ones. You can be playing poorly, but hitting one or two great shots will make you forget all the bad ones. *The intellect is the process, the emotions are the motivation, the product is the progression of one's game.*

It is hard to improve if all you care about is your score. Scoring for the high-handicapper should not be the objective, but the product of the process. Concentrate on developing the process: good golfing habits, a positive mental approach and a consistent pre-shot routine. Hitting good shots should be your objective. Don't work on changing your swing in the middle of your round; that can be done later at the range. When you're swinging the club well and hitting good shots, the scoring will automatically come.

CHAPTER TEN

POWER GOLF
Hitting the Long Ball

Every player wants to hit the long ball and rightfully so. It improves the whole game and makes it a lot more fun. Having good length off the tee sets up the rest of the hole to play shorter, which means you have a better chance to shoot a lower score. Also, hitting a long powerful drive gives you confidence with the rest of your game as well as impressing or intimidating your competitors.

First understand that you do not have to be big and strong, nor do you have to be an Olympic athlete to hit the long drive. One of the longest drivers in golf is a young college kid named Tiger Woods. Tiger is just 20 years old and weighs in at around 160 pounds soaking wet. He has won the last two U.S. Amateur golf tournaments and has been compared to a young Jack Nicklaus. His drives routinely soar well over 300-yards and have been the subject of folklore around the circuit. Fans follow him just to marvel at his distance, watching him hit a 9-iron for his second shot on a par 5. Tiger has the rare ability to hit his drives high with little spin. This gives him maximum carry and roll. His secret is not brute strength, but perfect form, optimal timing and the proper mindset. As in the martial arts, power is generated by form and timing, and speed is generated by the proper mindset. To gain distance off the tee, you must prepare yourself both physically and mentally.

PHYSICAL PREPARATION

Physical preparation is about preparing your body and your equipment. The best thing you can do for your body is to become flexible. Power is developed from the lower body through the upper body. The resistance created between the hips and the shoulders has a large effect on how fast the upper body unwinds around the lower body. The larger the differential between the twisting shoulders and the hips, the greater distance your drives will travel. Chapter Two of this book is devoted to stretching exercises that will help you gain this much needed flexibility.

Now let's look at your equipment. Even though distance is largely dictated by your swing, having the proper equipment will optimize your efforts (much of this is covered in Chapter Four). There are three things you can examine to help you gain distance off the tee:

1. *The clubhead size, material and loft angle:* One key to gaining distance off the tee is to hit the ball on the sweet

spot of the club. This is where oversize drivers can be a benefit to most amateurs. With the advent of metal heads, manufacturers can produce a larger headed club that has a larger sweet spot. Even mishit balls travel farther off an oversize club than a standard sized one. Also, pay attention to the loft angle of the club. The old myth, the less loft the greater the distance is not true. The ball comes off the clubface at a different angle for a player who possesses a high clubhead speed versus a player with a low clubhead speed. It also depends on from what angle the clubhead contacts the ball. If you have a swing arc that is more upright and hit the ball on the upswing, you'll get more distance from a less lofted driver. If you have a flatter swing, you'll get better results with a more lofted club. Players with slow swing speed may benefit more from a more lofted driver (13 to 15 degrees) which helps get the ball up in the air. Also, don't forget about how the center of gravity affects the balls flight. Finding the right clubhead and loft is a function of trial and error.

2. *The club shaft, its length, flex rating and weight:* With the technological advances in materials, the driver can be made longer and lighter. Not long ago, a standard driver was approximately 43 inches long with a 115 to 120 gram steel shaft, and a grip weighing about 50 grams. Today, we can find graphite shafted drivers up to 48 inches long with a shaft weight of around 60 grams, and a grip weight of 32 grams. With a longer and lighter shaft, you can swing the club much faster. The longer shaft increases the arc radius creating a higher clubhead speed. But a club that is too light can bring about swing flaws because of the loss of feel in the club. The longer shaft also magnifies any swing flaws as the increased length makes the club harder to control. The key is to buy the longest shaft that you can control. Here are a few points to remember when looking for a driver:

- When testing longer shafted drivers, you defeat the purpose if you fail to make consistent solid contact with the ball.

- Buy the softest shaft that you can control. The softer the shaft, the more kick the shaft will generate. (Refer to p. 69 for more on club shafts).

3. *The spin rate of the balls:* Go with low spin balls instead of the high spin varieties. A low spin ball generally flies straighter and longer than a high spin ball. You have to determine if sacrificing control around the greens is worth the extra distance you will gain off the tee. If you're the type of player who has a hard time staying in the fairway off the tee, you definitely should go with the low spin ball.

When all is said and done, the real key to getting distance from your equipment is to hit the ball squarely. You can have the most technically innovative driver ever made, but if you don't hit the sweet spot and hit it square, you will have wasted a lot of money.

MENTAL PREPARATION

Don't hit the ball, swing through it! The hit impulse probably ruins more drives than any other swing thought. When you try to hit the ball, the natural tendency is to cast your club at the ball violently with your hands and arms. This *hit impulse* not only tenses up the muscles, but it also negates all the power that was built up in your lower body. This is the single hardest thing for a high-handicapper to do. Every player wants to hit the ball hard, so everyone thinks the harder they swing, the greater the clubhead speed. *Wrong!* Remember the martial arts lesson, *speed is developed from lack of muscle tension.*

Remember the times when you just swung the club easily and hit the ball a ton? You said to yourself, ***Boy, I barely swung!*** Well, chances are you did just that. A very free and loose swing with a relaxed body generates more speed and consistency in your swing. It is very hard to convince anyone that swinging at eighty percent produces more clubhead speed than swinging at one-hundred percent. To demonstrate it to yourself, pick up a baseball and throw it two different ways:

- First, grip the ball hard tensing your muscles. Then try to throw the ball as hard and far as you can.

- Secondly, pick up the ball and hold it in your fingers. Now, with a relaxed whipping motion, throw the ball as far as you can keeping your arm fairly relaxed.

What happens? If you're like most, the second ball travels considerably farther with more velocity. Think about what you just did. You generated power for that throw by winding your upper body around your lower body. Think about how a baseball pitcher throws a 100 mph fastball over the plate. Starting with a solid stance, he begins the windup by taking his arm back, turning the shoulders, resisting with the hips, and letting his weight transfer to the back foot. When he is completely coiled up, he starts the pitch by unwinding his body in the exact opposite sequence of his windup. He begins the pitch by stepping forward with the left foot and unwinding his hips, followed by his shoulders, and then arms. As his weight fully transfers to the front foot, his arm whips through with his wrist unloading at the last second. Because he is relaxed when he allows his body to uncoil, he can focus on the target. In baseball this motion is called *a pitch;* in karate it is called *a cobra strike;* in golf it is called *a golf swing.*

If you look at high speed film of the clubface contacting the ball, you will see the ball flatten against the clubface, ride the face for a brief second, then spring off the clubface. I'll call the area where the ball stays in contact with the clubface, *the power zone.* You have to remember that the ball doesn't go from zero to 100 plus miles per hour instantly; it accelerates parabolically in a millisecond. The longer you can keep the clubface on the ball, the farther the ball travels. This is why it is so important to keep the club accelerating through the power zone. With a hit impulse, all energy is relaxed after the hit. This allows the club to decelerate after initial contact. With a relaxed swing, the clubhead accelerates through the power zone.

Recently, I attended the AT&T Pebble Beach Pro Am in Monterey, California. The great thing about this unique tournament is that every foursome had two professional players and two celebrity/amateur players. Here, you got to marvel at the pros, then have fun with the celebs. This tournament is also unique in that it's played on three different courses over the span of four days with all players playing at Pebble Beach on the final day. On Thursday I went to Poppy Hills, a difficult hilly course inland on the Monterey Peninsula. The celebrities were there on that day so I was looking forward to my first experience at a pro event. I arrived at the fifteenth tee, a 210-yard par 3. I watched both pros and celebrities tee off. The first thing that jumped out at me when comparing the pros with the celebrities was that the *pros swing a lot easier.* I was amazed when Duffy Waldorf, a pro player and a very big guy, took out a 4-iron, swung almost in slow motion and knocked the ball stiff on the green. All the pro players had a smooth and easy swing, at least it looked that way. But from the distance they were hitting their balls, I knew they were generating a lot of clubhead speed. Whether they had a driver or an iron, the pros looked like they were swinging in slow motion, while the amateurs were swinging the way most amateurs do—*Violently with their arms!*

There was a good article entitled "57 Keys to Distance" in the February '96 issue of Golf Digest. The article featured quotes from different pros with their philosophies on distance. Some of my favorite were:

Ernie Els: "My main thought is to finish the backswing. That makes it easier to release the club through the ball."

Hal Sutton: "Wind up your shoulders as far as you can, then let it go."

Justin Leonard: "Make a little longer backswing, a little slower. Give it a little pause at the top so everything comes down together."

Woody Austin: "Remain relaxed."

Nick Price: "Bigger shoulder turn."

Payne Stewart: "I don't change my swing. I widen my stance a little."

Davis Love III: "Try to catch it solid. You'll get more distance if you swing at about 80 percent."

John Adams: "Try not to hit from the top. Make sure your club starts accelerating halfway into the downswing."

Bob Tway: "The main thing is not trying to hit too hard. Making a slower and bigger turn really helps a lot."

Kelly Robbins: "Try to swing at 80 to 90 percent. It's easier on your body and produces more yardage."

Chi Chi Rodriguez: "I just hit the hell out of it."

The common theme that most of the pros tell us is, *to not swing too hard.* It is far better to hit the ball square making solid contact, than to flail away with an all-out swing. In golf, as in karate, good technique will always defeat brute strength.

They also say, *don't get caught up with swing thoughts.* All practice should be at the range, all pre-shot thinking should be done behind the ball. When you step up and address the ball, just hit it!

LET YOUR POWER SWING MATCH YOUR BODY

First remember that a natural swing is complementary to body type. What works for some players won't always work for others. Power and speed are developed by good technique, but the techniques used will vary slightly from golfer to golfer. Being a long time karate instructor, I learned long ago that all students were different so the techniques I taught them varied slightly from student to student. Some were built like bears while others were built like cranes. Someone who is 6'2", 170 pounds is not going to move like a bear, while someone 5'10", 250 pounds is not going to float like a crane. Through the teachings, each student settled into the style that suited him or her best.

Mike Adams, one of Golf Magazine's top 100 teachers, wrote an article titled "Fit Your Swing to Your Physique" for the March '96 issue. After years of study, he grouped the pros swing into three categories:

1. Medium-built golfers with a good degree of flexibility are *leverage swingers.* A leverage swinger is characterized by a flat, around the body swing, an exaggerated hip turn, early hinging of the wrists, and a bending and straightening action of the right arm. A leverage swinger acts like a giant coil spring winding and unwinding. If you are a leverage swinger, work on developing the timing of the coiling and uncoiling of your body. Get the different leverages working for you, early hinging and late unhinging or arms and wrists. Power is developed from resistance between hip and shoulder turning. To generate more power in this swing, try speeding up the uncoiling of the hips and straightening of your right elbow.

2. A tall flexible golfer with long limbs is an *arc swinger.* Power is generated by creating a huge arc based on the

principle the greater the distance from the axis, the greater the speed. This swing is characterized by a long low takeaway to a backswing that takes the club back on a low and wide swing path. The result of standing tall at address with very little knee flex creates a big arc. If you are an arc swinger, work on generating speed by driving your legs and hips toward the target faster. The more you work the lower body, the faster the upper body responds.

3. A golfer with a thicker upper body and limited flexibility is a *width swinger*. Power is generated by a big shoulder turn and wide arc. It is important to maintain a solid base with a wide stance. To gain more power, work on a bigger shoulder turn and don't worry about taking the club back behind you. Try to turn your left shoulder past the ball and extend your arms and club away from the target. Your limited flexibility keeps you from doing otherwise. On the downswing, keep your lower body quiet with your feet flat on the ground. The big muscles of the upper body power the swing. Power is developed from the turning of the upper body over a quiet lower body.

Next is to highlight certain aspects of the natural golf swing you've learned to ensure that you develop the maximum clubhead possible. The concepts for a big tee shot are simple; *You build energy on the backswing, and you release that energy on the downswing!*

POWER TECHNIQUES

To hit the ball a great distance, you have to load and unload three things in your golf swing: the turning of your body, the swinging of your arms, and the cocking of your wrists. Depending how effective you are at all three, and the longer you can delay the unloading of the wrists, the farther the ball will go. A late wrist release ensures that the clubhead will be whipped through the golf ball at maximum velocity.   The timing of the release, set up by the tempo and rhythm of the swing is critical for the success for this shot. The wrists should release as the whole body unloads into the ball. But slicers beware; you will gain more distance by learning how to hit it straight rather than employing a late wrist release.

LATE WRIST RELEASE

RELEASE THE ENERGY!

The key to releasing the energy on your drive is not to think about it too much. A fluid swing motion is a natural swing uncluttered by techniques and swing thoughts. It's a two-fold process which is both technical and animalistic. The technical side is all the stuff before you actually step up to the ball. Everything from the setup position to the techniques you want to use during the swing. All of this thinking should be done behind the ball during your pre-shot routine. The animalistic side takes over when you step up to the ball. Your only concern is shooting at the target. Hitting the ball is instinctive.

Obtaining clubhead speed and power off the tee is not really that difficult as long as you don't try too hard, relax, and follow a few simple tips. When you get ready to tee off, stand behind the ball lining up your target. Visualize how you want to hit it; visualize the result. You've practiced your techniques at the range, so you know you are capable. Take a couple of practice swings emphasizing techniques you want to use such as; *turn the right hand over, good weight shift, etc.* Do all your thinking behind the ball. When you're ready, step up to the ball with one focus in mind, take a deep breath and *just do it!* You are no longer Mr.-Nice-Guy-Technical-Swing-Thoughts, you are Mr.-Just-Hit-the-Ball-Animalistic-Beast.

KEY POINTS

Setup Position: Spread your heels slightly wider and set your hands slightly behind the ball. This encourages a low takeaway and a wide swing arc on a shallow plane. Hitting the ball on a low plane sends the ball forward. Many beginners tend to hit the ball with a steep swing plane. This tends to hit the ball up and not out.

Ball Position: Play the ball up off the left heel. This ensures that you strike the ball with an upward swing.

Takeaway: Don't guide the club back; swing it back on a low trajectory and be careful not to pick the club up too soon. Guiding the club creates tension, swinging does not. A low takeaway helps create a big arc and a flat swing plane.

Backswing: Keep it slow and wide and try to stay relaxed. Let the weight naturally transfer over to the right side. Allow the wrists to fully cock forming an L.

Position at the Top: Shoulders should be fully turned with the left shoulder and knee behind the ball. Keep your left arm firm but not stiff. It is important to keep your hands up high. *Don't drop your hands behind your head.* This makes the club come over the top.

Downswing: Accelerate smoothly into the downswing and hit through the ball. Pick a spot along the target line beyond the ball to aim at. This helps take focus away from hitting the ball to making the swing. Begin with the hips and hold the L position or wrist cock as long as possible; this is the late release that all long hitters share.

Impact Position: Don't think about the "*hit*," just swing though the ball. Let the arms extend and make sure you allow the right hand to roll over.

Finish Position: Your hips and shoulders should be square to the target with ninety percent of your weight on your left foot.

Power Golf: Setup Position

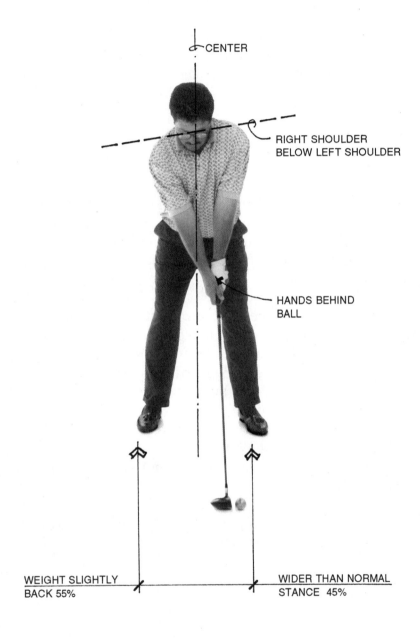

CENTER

RIGHT SHOULDER
BELOW LEFT SHOULDER

HANDS BEHIND
BALL

WEIGHT SLIGHTLY
BACK 55%

WIDER THAN NORMAL
STANCE 45%

Power Golf: Takeaway Position

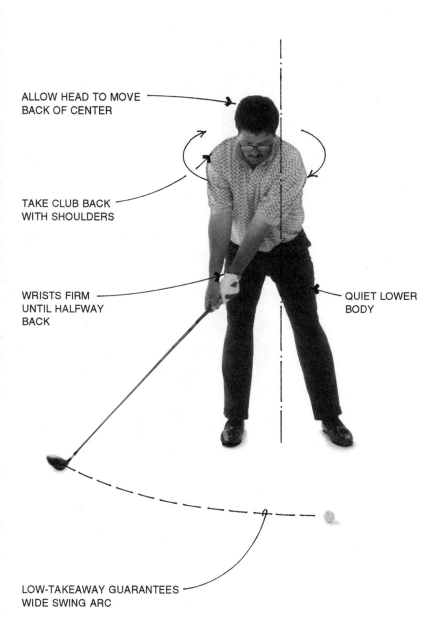

ALLOW HEAD TO MOVE
BACK OF CENTER

TAKE CLUB BACK
WITH SHOULDERS

WRISTS FIRM
UNTIL HALFWAY
BACK

QUIET LOWER
BODY

LOW-TAKEAWAY GUARANTEES
WIDE SWING ARC

Power Golf: Halfway Back

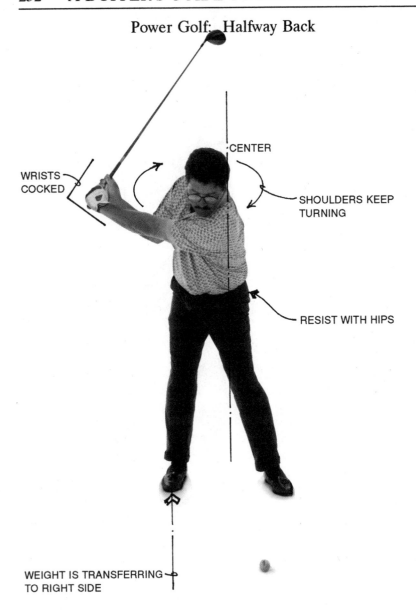

WRISTS
COCKED

CENTER

SHOULDERS KEEP
TURNING

RESIST WITH HIPS

WEIGHT IS TRANSFERRING
TO RIGHT SIDE

Power Golf: Position at the Top

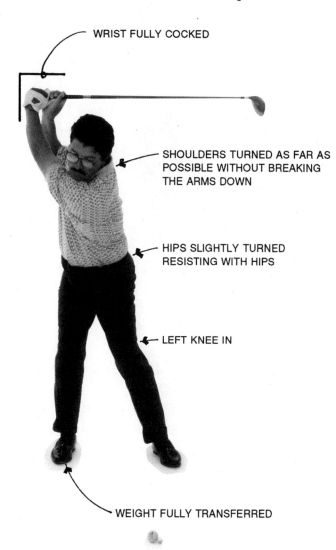

WRIST FULLY COCKED

SHOULDERS TURNED AS FAR AS
POSSIBLE WITHOUT BREAKING
THE ARMS DOWN

HIPS SLIGHTLY TURNED
RESISTING WITH HIPS

LEFT KNEE IN

WEIGHT FULLY TRANSFERRED

Power Golf: Downswing

SHOULDERS FOLLOW HIPS

RIGHT ELBOW &
SHOULDER DROP
DOWN

WRISTS STAY
COCKED

INITIATE SWING
WITH HIPS

WEIGHT STARTS TO TRANSFER
TO THE LEFT SIDE

Power Golf: Impact Position

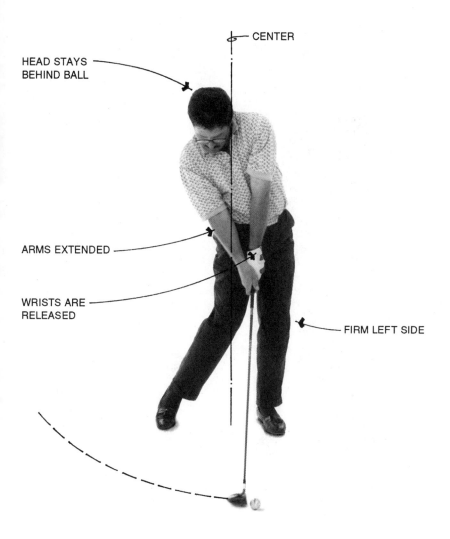

CENTER

HEAD STAYS
BEHIND BALL

ARMS EXTENDED

WRISTS ARE
RELEASED

FIRM LEFT SIDE

Power Golf: Extension Through Impact

STAY BEHIND CENTER

KEEP ARMS EXTENDED
THROUGH IMPACT

KEEP LEFT
SIDE FIRM

Power Golf: Follow-Through

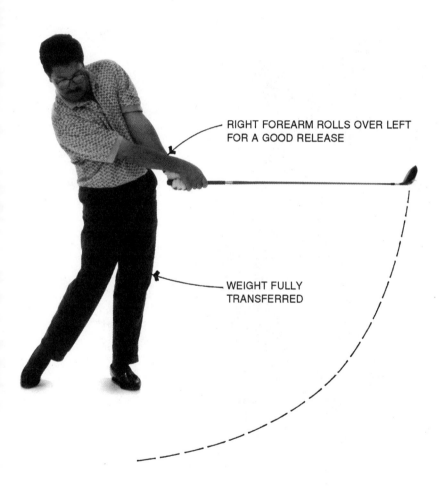

RIGHT FOREARM ROLLS OVER LEFT
FOR A GOOD RELEASE

WEIGHT FULLY
TRANSFERRED

Power Golf: Finish Position

CLUB FINISHES BEHIND HEAD

RIGHT SHOULDER

ALIGN

HIPS SQUARE TO TARGET

ALIGN

LEFT KNEE STRAIGHT

ALIGN

TOP OF FOOT 90% OF WEIGHT

ON RIGHT TOE

CHAPTER ELEVEN

DUFFER FAULTS
Techniques to Avoid

In search of a good golf swing, most beginners either try to teach themselves or take lessons from friends. Unfortunately, most friends are not qualified to give lessons, so the student may end up with a lot of misguided information. Golfers seem to be very susceptible to misinformation; if they hear something or read something they will try it. They'll listen to anyone with some well-meaning advice. This is dangerous because what works for some might not work for others. There are an over-abundance of swing theories out there that can clutter your mind. All players are looking for shortcuts to that great swing, and the first step to getting there is to throw away all the swing thoughts and myths you don't need.

Myth 1: Keep your left arm straight. Attempting to keep your left arm straight only introduces tension that inhibits your swing. If your left arm is too stiff, it may be hard to drop your arm inside which is essential for making an inside-out swing.

It's better to say:
Keep your left arm firm: A firm left arm does not collapse on the backswing, but still allows the arms and shoulders to rotate on the proper plane. Concentrate on keeping the arm firm and don't worry if it bends a little. Just remember the arm will be extended at impact.

Myth 2: Keep your head down: It is impossible to make a good shoulder turn with your chin buried in your chest. Many players, in an effort to keep their head down, dip their head on the backswing, then raise it up on the forwardswing. This ultimately changes your spine angle during the middle of your swing which changes your swing plane.

It's better to say:
Keep your head up: Keeping your head up allows for an easier rotation of your shoulders under your chin. It also keeps your spine straight and keeps your swing on plane.

Myth 3: Keep your head still: As your shoulders turn back, your head naturally wants to shift back. Keeping your head still on the backswing prevents your weight from properly shifting to the right leg. If your weight is allowed to stay on your left foot, your swing plane will come in too steep causing a *heavy* or *chunked shot.*

It's better to say:
Keep your head level: Allowing your head to shift back automatically shifts your weight properly. The proper weight shift from front to back to front is essential for creating power and accuracy in your shot.

Myth 4: Swing slowly for power: Swinging too slow causes you to guide the club back rather than swinging the club back. Too deliberate of a swing creates tension and negates all power from leverage that is created from a free swinging swing.

It is better to say:
Swing smoothly for power: Violently jerking or casting the club produces speed where it is not needed. A smooth tempo allows the club to build speed to a maximum at impact.

Myth 5: Make a bigger turn for power: Most players attempting to make a bigger turn don't really turn their shoulders much more, they overswing with their arms. *Just because John Daly can do it doesn't mean you can.*

It is better to say:
Turn as far as you can while keeping your hands high: By keeping your hands high, you lose the tendency to drop them behind your head. Classic over-swingers bend their arms behind their head which allows the club to hang down. The shaft of the club should never go past parallel to the ground. If it does, it will be very difficult to get the club back on plane.

Myth 6: Line the feet to the target: This misalignment gets many golfers into trouble. Next time you go to the range, pick a target and line your feet as you normally would. Take your club and lay it on the ground behind you touching both heels. Now step back and see where the club is pointing. If you're like most beginners, the club is pointing to the right. It is important to realize that if you align your feet to the target, they will not be parallel with the ball's target line. In fact, you will be aligned to the right of the target. When you make a swing with this alignment, you naturally come over the top in an effort to hit the ball toward the target.

It is better to say:

Align yourself parallel to the target line: You have to get used to properly aligning yourself. A good drill is to pick a target, tee your ball low, then place another tee a couple of feet down the target line. Next, lay a club down on the ground toward your feet parallel with the ball and tee. Then lay a club down perpendicular to the first club with the handle pointing at the ball. This helps you to see the proper alignment of your feet to the intended target.

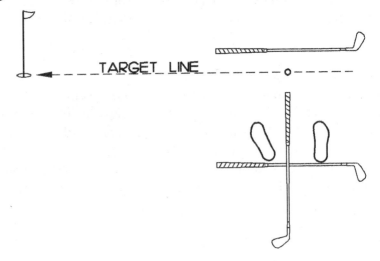

TARGET LINE

ALIGNMENT DRILL

A set-up guaranteed to ruin your swing!

Hands too far forward: This position causes the club to be picked up too steeply making a very narrow swing arc. This open alignment cause an out-to-in swing path creating a pull or pull-slice.

Corrected stance: The butt of the club should be pointing to the inside of your left thigh.   This allows the club to stay low on the takeaway creating that big arc. Your feet, hips and shoulders should be parallel to the target.

Backswing that guarantees a weak shot!

Left arm above the right: Allowing your arms and hands to control the backswing usually results in pulling the club too far inside. This results in a flat swing plane with a small arc. To hit the ball, you have to flick the club down with your wrists.

Correction, keep the left arm low: Let the shoulders create the swing path while the arms maintain their position. This allows the body to properly wind up.

Downswing that guarantees a hook or pulled-slice!

Club outside of swing plane: When the hands take over, the tendency is to bring the club over the top. It is now impossible to let your weight transfer forward. Instead your right knee pushes out making the angle of attack even more out-to-in. You will hit a big hook or a pull-slice.

Corrected swing plane: By starting the downswing with your lower body, the arms naturally pull to the inside dropping the club into the proper plane.

The Reverse Pivot

Collapsing the left knee or dipping your left shoulder causes the body's weight to stay over the left foot. This leads to many problems. Most of the power in the swing is lost due to improper weight shift and the steep angle of the swing path makes it hard to square the club. If your weight stays too far forward, you'll hit a heavy shot. If your weight stays back, you'll hit the shot thin.

Left foot drill: Pointing your left foot toward the target keeps your knees from collapsing. This allows your weight to shift properly when your shoulders are rotating around your hips. Concentrate on starting the downswing with your hips. This starts everything moving inside. I've seen people put a beach ball between their legs to keep the knees from collapsing. Unfortunately, most players don't carry beach balls in their bag.

Problem: *The Block:*   This happens when you hit a straight shot that immediately takes off to the right.   This can be caused by a multitude of things, but the most common is failure to release the right hand.

The Fix: *The Split-Grip Drill:*   A good way to ensure that your hands are turning over, is to grip a middle iron with your hands about 6 inches apart.   Make an easy swing and notice how your hands naturally turn over.

Problem: *Still Blocking Shots:*
There is a great drill which forces
you to turn your hands over and
draw the ball. Choke down on a
club. Then, taking the clubhead
way inside, swing through with the
body trying to keep the arms in
tight. Feel as if you're trying to
pull the butt of the club into the
front of your left thigh. I used to
worry about pulling the butt in too
close, but the momentum of the
swing will not allow you to do that.

Pulling the club toward your thigh
on the downswing quickly squares
up the clubface causing you to hit
straight or a slight draw.

Problem: *The Flying Elbow:* This is one of the biggest reasons that high-handicappers have a hard time squaring the club. When the elbow flies open, it keeps the hands ahead of the ball making it virtually impossible to turn the club over.

The Fix: *The Dollar-Bill Drill:* A good way to ensure that your elbow stays in, is to slip a dollar bill under your left arm. When you make a full swing, try to keep the bill from falling to the ground. This helps force the right hand to turn over the left.

The Problem: *The Pop-Up:* This happens when the ball is teed-up and you make a swing with a wood. The ball goes straight up with very little distance. Evidence of the club sliding under ball is usually evident with a mark on top of your clubhead. This is most likely caused by allowing your body to slide forward instead of turning.

The Fix: Try putting a stick into the ground right next to you between your left leg and the target. Make your regular swing and try to complete your turn inside the stick.

When you make the turn inside the stick, you should not have slid forward. If you knock the stick over or crash into it, you have slid forward. Try to complete the follow thru within the confines of the stick and finish in balance.

The Problem: *The Chunk or Hitting Fat:* This occurs when the club hits the ground behind the ball digging in and scrubbing off speed or bouncing the blade into the ball. This can be caused by many things but usually occurs due to too much of your arms and hands involved in the swing. It also occurs if you fail to clear your left hip making you cast the club at the ball.

The Fix: *The Headcover Drill:* Place your headcover about 12 to 18 inches behind the ball. Make your normal swing, but miss the headcover as you hit the ball. After you've hit your headcover a few times, you will realize the only possible way to properly hit the ball while missing the headcover is to properly shift your weight. A good weight shift to the left foot brings the clubhead in on the proper angle.

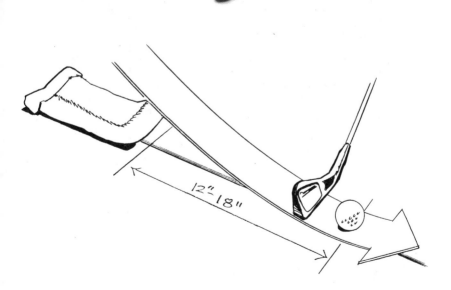

The Problem: *The Worm Burner:* Everyone has hit the shot that skips and runs along the ground. This is almost always caused by one of two things. Either you've kept your weight on your back foot, or you've hurried the downswing in an effort to hit the ball hard. When beginners swing hard, they tend to pull the club up with their hands in an effort to help get the ball in the air.

The Fix: Make a nice easy swing with a ball under the outside of your right foot. This keeps you from rolling your weight on the outside of your back foot. Once your weight gets to the outside, it is hard to bring it back.

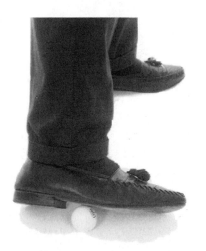

CHAPTER TWELVE

THE TAO OF GOLF
Lessons We Learned

Golf is for all ages. It is perhaps the only sport where youth and stature have little advantage over age and experience. Golf forces the armchair athlete to exercise on the field of battle while reminding him or her that it is fun to compete. It is an outlet for stress that reminds the workaholic what it was like to play again. Golf is still only a game.

Knowledge is a building block to learning; experience is the application of the knowledge; optimism is an attitude achieved through experience; rewards are begotten from progression. The lessons that you have learned will not only help your golf game progress, but will help enhance your everyday life.

Preparation

A warrior going to battle has the advantage if properly prepared.
Proper preparation of your equipment, body, and mind makes
you a better golfer.

- When your clubs are tuned to your swing they won't be a
  detriment to your game, but an asset to your psyche. You
  won't have to constantly adjust your swing for the
  deficiencies of your equipment, but let your equipment
  work with the swing that is natural for you.

- When your body is in golf shape, your game is not limited
  by your own physical shortcomings. Flexibility and a
  strong base are keys to hitting powerful drives. Relaxation
  and tempo are keys for good shotmaking. The golf swing
  is an athletic move; proper preparation enhances the
  efficiency of the swing. When your body is properly
  prepared, good things come to you.

- Mental preparation is essential to consistent shotmaking.
  Concentration should be focused toward the target, not on
  the swing. When errant swing thoughts enter our mind,
  our attention shifts to the swing which is counter-
  productive to achieving the objective, better scores. High-
  handicappers focus their energies on the swing, low-
  handicappers focus on scoring. When your mind is
  focused, your confidence is high. A combatant without
  confidence has already lost before he has begun.

Goals

A contest has no meaning unless there is a prize at the end. It is so important to set a goal and achieve that goal for the sense of accomplishment it provides for you. In this way, you have something with which to build your confidence, therefore your game.

- Set goals for your practice sessions. Once these goals have been reached, leave. It is better to end your practice on a positive note knowing that you have accomplished everything you set out to do. The goal of a practice session has never been merely to finish hitting your $5 bucket of balls.

- Remember, you are not yet a scratch golfer so don't worry if you fail to shoot par. Set a realistic personal par for the course you are about to play, and achieve your goal. At least then, your goal is clearcut and achievable.

- Set immediate, short-term and long-term goals. As each goal is conquered, you gain confidence that carries you through to the next level.

Knowledge

Knowledge is power; when you have knowledge, you learn how to correct problems, not agonize over them. Knowledge gained through teachings and experience are the basis for the improvement of your game. When you are committed toward a certain goal, and ready to work toward that goal, the knowledge you possess helps make the changes required to attain those goals. Your brain is a storehouse of knowledge; it takes in information, dissects it, assimilates it, organizes it, implements it, then learns from it. *This is the human learning process.*

- *Information:* You gather information by taking lessons, reading books, watching videos, listening to friends, and so forth. You absorb information from any and all sources that surround you.

- *Dissection:* Your brain quickly scans the information, sorts out what is relevant and of interest, then categorizes and prioritizes the information based on what you are trying to achieve.

- *Assimilation:* You take what you've learned, keep the good, store the bad, then combine it with what you already know. The new information gained is stored and continually tested.

- *Organization:* Taking the knowledge you've learned and making a plan on how to achieve your goals. By making goals, you are making a plan for improvement.

- *Implementation:* Once you have the understanding of the information, you can take steps to implement the knowledge you have gained.

Attitude

The state of the athlete's mind as he faces his event determines the degree of excess tension he will carry into the event. The athlete free from excess tension as he awaits his performance is typically self-confident. He has what is commonly known as "a winning attitude." 5

- A positive attitude does more for your progress and enjoyment of the game of golf. By emphasizing the positive and not dwelling on the negative, you find more enjoyment than frustration in the game.

- Find something good in every shot. So what if you topped the ball, at least it rolled straight. Realize that even the top pros sometimes hit errant shots. Be your own best friend.

- Good luck always outweighs bad luck. Keep in mind that you are bound to get unlucky once in a while on the golf course. But more times than not, good luck is more prevalent than bad. Soon you forget the shot that bounced off a tree and landed on the green.

- Stay in the present. Don't dwell on the bad shots and avoid counting the good ones before they happen. A sure fire way to destroy a good round, is to end with a few bad holes thinking of what could have been.

5: Bruce Lee, Tao of Jeet Kune Do (Ohara Publications, Copyright 1975)

Character

Playing golf with someone reveals more about his or her character that you may ever intend to know. Golf has a way of bringing out the best and worst in a person. You think you know someone until you play a round of golf with him or her. Character flaws magnified during a round of golf may remain hidden otherwise.

- *The Whiner:* This guy moans and complains about every bad shot he makes. If it's not the course, it's his equipment or some kind of distraction, it's never his fault. You can usually hear him cussing from the other fairways. If you play with this guy, throw a bottle of aspirins in your bag.

- *Mr. Armchair Expert:* This player knows everything about golf, or seems to; anything you've done, he's done it before. He always has some advice for you on improving your game. He can easily quote a famous pro or something he's read. His bag is stocked with the latest and hottest clubs on the market. He is fun to play with because he is good natured and only trying to help.

- *Mr. Big Ego:* This guy always has to win; if he doesn't he always has an excuse as to why not. Being the longest driver is most important to him. He rarely plays with people whom he cannot beat. He usually has a hard time keeping track of his own score, but watches everyone elses closely. He moves his ball when nobody is looking and rarely compliments anyone's good shots. I try to avoid playing with this guy.

Golf is also a great way to build character. It is probably the only major sport that is founded on honesty. Players are expected to, and routinely do, call penalties upon themselves. But at the same time, there is probably more habitual cheating that takes place during a round than any other sport. Playing with women is a good way for men to measure their own attitude and character. There's nothing more devastating to the male psyche than being beat by a woman.

When men play with women, their egos always try to impress them with the distance of their tee shots. This over-swinging produces a 300-yard drive: 200 yards out and 100 yards to the right. Most women do not hit the ball as far as men, but they always hit it straight. When playing with women, I find that even though I can hit the ball farther, I am so busy trying to get back to the fairway that the advantage gained off the tee is lost. We would end up on the green with the same number of shots. Luckily, I barely won the game. *Whew!*

Balance

Having balance in one's life is the most important ingredient to a long and happy life. Most everyone gets too caught up in trying to earn that elusive buck, and forgets how to have fun. It's important to one's health to get rid of excess stress and tension. It is doubly important to mix work and play in one's routine.

- *Golf promotes healthy play:* Adults tend to forget how to play games. Golf is a professional sport that pays millions of dollars, but is still essentially a game.

- *Golf rewards all players with occasional greatness:* Golf is the only sport where everyone can be rewarded with a great shot. Do you remember when you hit that perfect drive, or sank that long putt, the feeling you got from your accomplishment? It happens to all players, sooner or later.

- *Golf gathers together great friends in a beautiful setting:* Nothing is more fun than being with good friends and playing the game in a beautiful setting.

Life is short; people don't realize it until it is too late. When someone close to you passes away, you find yourself wishing you had spent more time with him or her, or you wonder what you *could have done to make their life more complete. After they are gone, it is too late.* **Live—life—everyday.**

CONCLUSIONS

Golf is fast becoming one of the most popular sports in the world. It comes as no surprise to those who have experienced even moderate success as to the reasons why. Golf can be enjoyed by men and women of all ages, of various ethnic and economical backgrounds. Just about anyone who can pick up a club can play golf. You do not have to be a great athlete to play golf, only a willing one. Golf offers no advantage to men over women, nor age versus youth. The handicapping system used in golf allows lesser players to compete with better players, thereby creating friendly competition. It is a game that if you cheat, you will only be cheating yourself.

Golf is a great way to meet people. When you show up at a golf course alone, the pro shop can match you up with up to three other players. When I was vacationing in San Diego last year, I wanted to play Torrey Pines. No one in my group was able to play that day, so I went down to the course alone. The starter immediately matched me up with three other individuals. Tom was an assistant manager of a restaurant in Atlanta, William was a bank auditor from New York, and Cathy was a sales rep from Washington.   Here were four complete strangers, talking and having a good time the entire afternoon. Our common bond was that we all loved to play golf.

The first professional golf tournament I attended, the AT&T Pebble Beach Pro Am in Monterey, California was a memorable experience and certainly won't be the last. This particular event is more than a golf tournament, it is a social gathering. It seems that most people were there to watch the celebrities rather than the pros.   In talking with other spectators, I learned that no other PGA event is like this one. This event, with it's amateur and celebrity players, encourages crowd participation.   Well; as far as PGA events allow. During the course of the tournament, I found myself following the celebrities more than the pros. The pros were always in the middle of the fairway, they rarely missed greens, and they almost never hit the ball out of bounds. Even though I was in awe of the pros, I enjoyed watching the celebs much more because they joked with the crowds and displayed human-like golf skills. I think most spectators felt this way because the largest crowds followed the celebrities. Bill Murray attracted by far the largest crowds, even larger than the legendary Jack Nicklaus. It was like watching the Pied Piper of Golf lead his subjects through the forests of Poppy Hills. Kevin Costner was acting like Mr. Cool on Thursday even though his last movie bombed. I understand he is currently making a movie where he plays a professional golfer. He was much better on Friday and he definitely attracted the most females; I liked following him. I enjoyed James Woods. He was akin to your best friend on the course, someone you could sit down and have a beer with.   He was most accommodating to the spectators and went out of his way to get my friend Debbie, a picture with himself and his playing partner, Andy Garcia. Andy seemed quite uptight on Thursday, but he was fairly loosened up by Friday. I saw James hit a trash can with one of his drives while Clint Eastwood shanked one into the trees; that was something I could relate to.

The pro players approached each hole in a very serious demeanor. After all, they were playing for hundreds of thousands of dollars. The celebrities were having fun, and I think this is why I connected with them much more. I play golf to have fun and I play with people who I enjoy. With celebrities like Bill Murray constantly working the crowd, it's no wonder why this is such a popular event with spectators and an event that the most ardent traditionalists avoid. A few years ago, I read that Commissioner Dean Beman was considering banning Bill Murray because of his antics. There were also some traditionalists who thought his behavior had no place in a golf tournament. After experiencing this unique tournament, I have to say that Bill Murray is the freshest thing about the tournament and a big reason why so many non-golfers attend the event. I think what Bill brings to the tournament and why he is so popular is that he reminds amateur players of themselves when they play. Sure it is great watching the pros; the shots they hit and the skills they demonstrate are amazing. But most players can't relate to that; they can only envy it. I like it when Clint shanks one into a tree, when James hits his drive into a trash can, or when Kevin puts his approach shot into the crowd. All duffers do this. Here is an event where one can watch matinee idols having fun doing what duffers like to do, play golf with their friends.

Simple in concept but difficult in execution, golf is one sport that offers no advantage to youth and athleticism, but rewards patience and experience. Golf is a very social sport that promotes constant interaction throughout the game whereas most other sports have interaction before or after the event. It is one of the only sports where one can enjoy a hotdog and a beer during the middle of the event.

People who do not enjoy golf have probably never played the game as it was supposed to be played. Non-golfers will find it hard to understand the compulsion that golfers inherit to play the game. In the eyes of other athletes, golfers are the people who can't make it in other sports; they are too slow or too fat to excel at anything that takes talent. But golf is addictive, it keeps bringing players back to a game most struggle with and search for ways to improve themselves.

I know that I will never score an NFL touchdown, or run the 100-yard dash in nine seconds flat; but I do know that during a round of golf, *I am bound to hit a great shot.* On any given day no matter how bad you're playing, sometime during the round, you will always hit at least one or two great shots. It may be a 300-yard drive, an approach shot close to the pin, or sinking that 50-foot putt.

Golf will always give you a small sample of greatness which keeps you coming back for more.

AFTERWORD

We learn by doing—some things work for us while others don't. Golf is one of those enigmas that we make harder than it really is.

A Duffer's Guide to Better Golf can serve as a guide for the amateur golfer. In my years as a martial arts instructor, students were required to gain proficiency with their basic skills before being allowed to spar. In golf, most of us begin sparring before we have any basic skills. This book is designed to help the amateur player gain these skills to better prepare himself/herself for playing golf.

Remember why you play golf. Go out and enjoy playing a great game, with your best friends, in a beautiful setting. With a better understanding and a better attitude towards the game, you will *shoot lower scores and have a lot more fun*

David Iwanaga

INDEX

RESOURCES

Instructional

**The Golf University
at San Diego**
17550 Bernardo Oaks Drive
San Diego, CA 92128
(800) 426-0966

James Perez
USGTF Teaching Pro
2225 North Milburn
Fresno, CA 93722
(209) 432-9490

Books/Bibliography

The Tao of Jeet Kune Do
by Bruce Lee
Ohara Publications 1975
P.O. Box 918
Santa Clarita, CA 91380-9018

Advanced Golf
by Greg Norman
Charles E. Tuttle Company Inc.
1995 153 Milk Street
Boston, MA 02109

**How to Play Your Best Golf
All the Time**
by Tommy Armour
Simon & Schuster 1953
1633 Broadway
New York, NY 10019-6785

**Playing the Great Game of
Golf - Making Every Minute
Count** *by Ken Blanchard*
William Morrow and Company
New York 1992
Blanchard Family Partnership

Manual of Yoga Sessions
by Yogi Shalom
Published by YOM 1981
4538 N. Hayston
Fresno, CA 93726

Power Golf
by Ben Hogan
A.S. Barnes & Company 1948
New York

Golf Equipment

Tony's 19th Hole
Owner Tony Rojas
Islewood Golf Range
2225 North Milburn
Fresno, CA 93722

Saville Row Golf
Owners John & Diane Tudor
13220 Evening Creek Drive
Suite 105
San Diego, CA 92128

Magazine Articles

I have not attempted to cite all the authors and sources consulted in the writing of this book. To do so would require more space than is available. The following articles are important to my research and have taught me a lot about golf.

How to Find a Better Ball
by Chuck Cook
Golf Digest/December 1995

A Matter of Some Gravity
by Ed Weathers
Golf Digest/October 1995

Long and Strong is Wrong
by Dave Pelz
Golf Magazine/February 1996

How Sweet It Is!
by Dave Pelz
Golf Magazine/September 1995

How to Play Par Golf
by Peter Sanders/Lorin Anderson
Golf Magazine/January 1996

Fit Your Swing to Your Physique
by Mike Adams
Golf Magazine/March 1996

Fairways and Greens
by Rick Smith
Golf Magazine/August 1995

Make Your Swing Work
by Rick Smith
Golf Magazine/July 1994

The Power Primer
by John Huggan
Golf Digest/February 1996

57 Keys to Distance
Quotes by Tour Pros
Golf Digest/February 1996

Load—Unload—Explode
by Jim McLean
Golf Magazine/November 1995

More Distance, It's All in the Wrists
by A. J. Bonar
Golf Illustrated/July-August 1995

Stop!—Eliminate these four deadly shots from your game.
by Jim McLean
Golf Magazine/November 1994

What You Don't Need to Think About
by Hank Haney
Golf Digest/October 1995

Make Pro Contact with Your Irons
by Bobby Clampett
Golf Tips/March 1996

Sole Considerations
by Dave Pelz
Golf Magazine/January 1996

Consultants

Golf Model: **Jim Perez**
USGTF Teaching Pro
2225 North Milburn
Fresno, CA 93722
(209) 432-9490

Fitness Model: **Karen Gerdts**
c/o Author

Cover Artist/   **Steve Austin / Jeff Austin**
Illustrations: P.O. Box 25868
Fresno, CA 93729-5868
(209) 323-6939

Book Editing: **Gail Kearns**
825 E. Pedregosa Street #2
Santa Barbara, CA 93103
(805) 898-9941

Photographer: **Jim Koike**
2767 West Shaw #122
Fresno, CA 93711
(209) 225-1631

Order Form

♬ Fax orders: (209) 449-9872

✉ Postal orders: Eagle Publishing, P.O. Box 14118
Pinedale, CA 93650

☎ Phone orders: (209) 449-9872

é **On-line orders: eaglepub@psnw.com**

Name: _____

Address: _____

City: _____

State: _____ **Zip:** _____

Telephone: (_____) _____

Please send me ___ copies of *A Duffer's Guide to Better Golf.* I understand that I may return any book for a full refund—for any reason within 30 days of purchase.

_____ copies times $15.95 = _____

Sales tax: California residents add 7.75% _____
for books shipped in state.

Shipping: Add $3.00 for shipping U.S. _____
Postal Priority or $4.00 for air mail

                            Total ===========

Payment: ❏ **Check or Money Order**
❏ **Credit card:** ❏ **Visa**   ❏ **Mastercard**

Card number: _____
Name on card: _____
    expiration date: _____